D1088148

The Northern Renaissance

GREAT ARTISTS OF THE WESTERN WORLD

The Northern Renaissance

Albrecht Dürer

———❧———

Lucas Cranach

———❧———

Hans Holbein

———❧———

Pieter Bruegel

MARSHALL CAVENDISH · LONDON · NEW YORK · SYDNEY

Staff Credits

Editors	Clive Gregory LLB Sue Lyon BA (Honours)	**Picture Researchers**	Vanessa Fletcher BA (Honours) Flavia Howard BA (Honours) Jessica Johnson BA
Art Editors	Chris Legee BFA Kate Sprawson BA (Honours) Keith Vollans LSIAD	**Production Controllers**	Tom Helsby Alan Stewart BSc
Deputy Editor	John Kirkwood BSc (Honours)	**Secretary**	Lynn Smail
Sub-editors	Caroline Bugler BA (Honours), MA Sue Churchill BA (Honours) Alison Cole BA, MPhil Jenny Mohammadi Nigel Rodgers BA (Honours), MA Penny Smith Will Steeds BA (Honours), MA	**Editorial Director**	Maggi McCormick
		Publishing Manager	Robert Paulley BSc
		Managing Editor	Alan Ross BA (Honours)
Designers	Stuart John Julie Stanniland	**Consultant and Authenticator**	Sharon Fermor BA (Honours) Lecturer in the Extra-Mural Department of London University and Lecturer in Art History at Sussex University

Reference Edition Published 1988

Published by Marshall Cavendish Corporation
147 West Merrick Road
Freeport, Long Island
N.Y. 11520

Typeset by Litho Link Ltd., Welshpool
Printed and Bound by Dai Nippon
Printing Co., Hong Kong Ltd.

Library of Congress Cataloging-in-Publication Data

Main entry under title:

Great Artists of the Western World II.

Includes index.
  1. Artists – Biography. I. Marshall Cavendish Corporation.
N40.G774 1988   709'.2'2 [B]   88–4317
ISBN 0–86307–900–8 (set)

ISBN 0–86307–900–8 (set)
        0–86307–755–2 (vol)

Preface

Looking at pictures can be one of the greatest pleasures that life has to offer. Note, however, those two words 'can be'; all too many of us remember all too clearly those grim afternoons of childhood when we were dragged, bored to tears and complaining bitterly, through room after room of Italian primitives by well-meaning relations or tight-lipped teachers. It was enough to put one off pictures for life – which, for some of us, was exactly what it did.

For if gallery-going is to be the fun it should be, certain conditions must be fulfilled. First, the pictures we are to see must be good pictures. Not necessarily great pictures – even a few of these can be daunting, while too many at a time may prove dangerously indigestible. But they must be well-painted, by good artists who know precisely both the effect they want to achieve and how best to achieve it. Second, we must limit ourselves as to quantity. Three rooms – four at the most – of the average gallery are more than enough for one day, and for best results we should always leave while we are still fresh, well before satiety sets in. Now I am well aware that this is a counsel of perfection: sometimes, in the case of a visiting exhibition or, perhaps, when we are in a foreign city with only a day to spare, we shall have no choice but to grit our teeth and stagger on to the end. But we shall not enjoy ourselves quite so much, nor will the pictures remain so long or so clearly in our memory.

The third condition is all-important: we must know something about the painters whose work we are looking at. And this is where this magnificent series of volumes – one of which you now hold in your hands – can make all the difference. No painting is an island: it must, if it is to be worth a moment's attention, express something of the personality of its painter. And that painter, however individual a genius, cannot but reflect the country, style and period, together with the views and attitudes of the people among whom he or she was born and bred. Even a superficial understanding of these things will illuminate a painting for us far better than any number of spotlights, and if in addition we have learnt something about the artist as a person – life and loves, character and beliefs, friends and patrons, and the places to which he or she travelled – the interest and pleasure that the work will give us will be multiplied a hundredfold.

Great Artists of the Western World will provide you with just such an insight into the life and work of some of the outstanding painters of Europe and America. The text is informative without ever becoming dry or academic, not limiting itself to the usual potted biographies but forever branching out into the contemporary world outside and beyond workshop or studio. The illustrations, in colour throughout, have been dispensed in almost reckless profusion. For those who, like me, revel in playing the Attribution Game – the object of which is to guess the painter of each picture before allowing one's eye to drop to the label – the little sections on 'Trademarks' are a particularly happy feature; but every aficionado will have particular preferences, and I doubt whether there is an art historian alive, however distinguished, who would not find some fascinating nugget of previously unknown information among the pages that follow.

This series, however, is not intended for art historians. It is designed for ordinary people like you and me – and for our older children – who are fully aware that the art galleries of the world constitute a virtually bottomless mine of potential enjoyment, and who are determined to extract as much benefit and advantage from it as they possibly can. All the volumes in this collection will enable us to do just that, expanding our knowledge not only of art itself but also of history, religion, mythology, philosophy, fashion, interior decoration, social customs and a thousand other subjects as well. So let us not simply leave them around, flipping idly through a few of their pages once in a while. Let us read them as they deserve to be read – and welcome a new dimension in our lives.

John Julius Norwich is a writer and broadcaster who has written histories of Venice and of Norman Sicily as well as several works on history, art and architecture. He has also made over twenty documentary films for television, including the recent Treasure Houses of Britain series which was widely acclaimed after repeated showings in the United States.

Lord Norwich is Chairman of the Venice in Peril Fund, and member of the Executive Committee of the British National Trust, an independently funded body established for the protection of places of historic interest and natural beauty.

John Julius Norwich

Contents

Introduction

As with the word 'Renaissance' itself, the term 'Northern Renaissance' is not susceptible to precise definition. In its broadest sense it is sometimes applied to virtually all European art outside Italy in the 15th and 16th centuries, functioning more as a convenient period label than as a stylistic category. Certainly there was a remarkable flowering of art in Northern Europe soon after 1400 (in some ways as momentous as the achievements of the great Florentine artists of the same period), most notably in the work of the painter Jan van Eyck and the sculptor Claus Sluter, each of whom introduced a revolutionary type of naturalism. However, the idea that is held to be central to the concept of the Renaissance – the revival and emulation of the culture and art of antiquity – had little influence outside Italy until the beginning of the 16th century. Thus the term 'Northern Renaissance' is often applied in a narrower sense to art outside Italy from about 1500, when the glamorous achievements south of the Alps began to be reflected in other countries. It is in this more restricted sense that the term is used in this volume.

During the early 16th century it became common for northern artists to visit Italy as part of their artistic education. The ways in which they responded to the wonders of ancient and modern art they saw there varied greatly. A few remained unmoved, but most of them clearly showed the impact of Italy in their work. However, only a handful of northern artists was completely successful in synthesizing the sharpness of observation and particularity of detail that were part of their heritage with the breadth and dignity of form characteristic of Italian Renaissance art.

The Northern Genius

The first and most important artist to achieve this distinction was Albrecht Dürer, the supreme genius of the Northern Renaissance. Dürer was such a commanding figure not only because of the quality of his work, but also because of the force of his intellect and personality. At the time when he was coming to maturity, German art was totally estranged from the spirit of the Renaissance, for late-Gothic art in his country was characteristically extravagant and mystical in a way that was entirely alien to the ideals of clarity, harmony and order associated with classical art. Single-handedly Dürer changed the direction of art in his country through his championing of the culture of the South. And

because he was primarily an engraver rather than a painter, his work achieved wide circulation through his prints, and he was a stimulus to artists all over Northern Europe, not just in Germany.

From the very beginning of his career Dürer stood apart from contemporary German artists, for although he was brought up in a tradition of great manual skill by his goldsmith father and his teacher, Michael Wolgemut, the influence of intellectual contacts was just as important, helping him to see the role of the artist as that of a creative thinker rather than merely the master of a craft. In his wide intellectual interests and high conception of the artist's calling, Dürer has often been compared with his great Italian contemporary Leonardo da Vinci, the supreme artist-thinker of the era and the virtual creator of the idea of the artist as genius.

Dürer twice visited Italy (1494-95 and 1505-07) and by the time of his second journey was a celebrated figure himself, who was treated with respect by the leading artists he met. Dürer's insatiable visual and intellectual curiosity and his great powers of synthesis led him to incorporate various aspects of Italian art in his work. His nude figures (p.20) show his concern with ideal systems of proportion, but he was also deeply affected by the sensuous richness of Venetian art, and it is a measure of his attainment that his Feast of the Rose Garlands (p.30), which was actually painted in Venice, was considered a resounding success even in the city whose painters were the widely acknowledged masters of colour.

A Unique Vision

Although his pre-eminence is undisputed, Dürer lived in a golden age for German painting and some of his contemporaries are major figures not only in German but in world art. Among them, Lucas Cranach is not only one of the most eminent painters but also one of the most instructive figures in showing the personal transmutations that took place in the spread of Renaissance ideals. Unlike Dürer, Cranach never visited Italy, but like Dürer he moved in intellectual circles, and the world of classical learning was part of the background against which he worked. Few artists of the period, indeed, painted such enchanting scenes of classical mythology, and although Cranach's figures – in their very slim proportions and quirky expressivenesss – are far removed from the ideals of ancient art, they yet rely on classical and

Renaissance prototypes. His marvellously winsome goddesses in his depictions of **The Judgement of Paris** (pp.54-5), for example, derive ultimately from ancient statues of **The Three Graces**, and his reclining nudes (pp.66-7) are based on a type made popular in Venice in the early 16th century by Giorgione and Titian.

Perfection in Portraiture

Cranach's work is remarkable not only for its quality and originality, but also for its extent and variety. Some of his finest achievements are portraits, but in this field he – like all other artists of the Northern Renaissance – yields the palm to his countryman, Hans Holbein the Younger. In his early career Holbein's work also was very varied; he painted religious works and large-scale secular decorations as well as portraits and also designed woodcuts, but his extraordinary sharp powers of observation were deployed most memorably in scrutinizing the human face, and it is as a portraitist – one of the greatest of any age or country – that he has achieved immortality.

Holbein was born in Augsburg, a city that had particularly close trading links with Italy, and

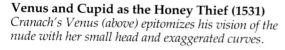

Venus and Cupid as the Honey Thief (1531)
Cranach's Venus (above) epitomizes his vision of the nude with her small head and exaggerated curves.

The artists
(top, left to right) Self-portrait by Holbein; a self-portrait by Dürer; (bottom, left to right) Bruegel by Bartholomeus Spranger; self-portrait by Cranach.

when he moved to Basle he formed a close friendship with the great humanist scholar Erasmus, who had an important influence on his career, not least in giving him a letter of introduction to Sir Thomas More in England, the main scene of his activity as a portraitist. There is no certain evidence that Holbein visited Italy, but it is generally believed that he did so around 1518. The impact of Italian art made his work more grand and lucid, as in The Meyer Madonna (p.90), which particularly shows the influence of Raphael. In this work and, for example, in the portrait of Mary Wotton, Lady Guildford (p.91) Renaissance features can be seen in the classical architectural forms as well as in the clarity and grandeur of the compositions.

Portraits such as this – with their astonishing sense of actuality and physical presence – must have been regarded with something akin to wonder in England, which at the time of Holbein's first visit was still largely medieval in its attitudes to art. A few Italian or other foreign artists had previously visited England, notably the sculptor Pietro Torrigiano (famous for breaking Michelangelo's nose), who made the tomb of Henry VII in Westminster Abbey, but their work had had little influence. Holbein, on the other hand, revolutionized painting (even though he had no worthy successors apart from the miniaturist Nicholas Hilliard) and he also introduced the Renaissance repertoire of decorative forms in his many designs for applied art. More than any other artist he brought the Renaissance to England.

An Atypical Master

Although the Netherlands are also fairly remote geographically from Italy, the Renaissance was taken up there with much greater alacrity than in England. Indeed, so many Netherlandish artists visited Italy and brought back Italian ideas to their country that the term 'Romanist', as applied to them, is of very frequent occurrence in the art historical literature on the period. It is, however, totally inappropriate to the greatest Netherlandish artist of the 16th century, Pieter Bruegel, who was wholly atypical in his relationship with Italy and Italian art. Bruegel made a fairly lengthy journey to Italy (the round trip probably lasted about two years and he went as far south as Sicily), but unlike most of his countrymen he was unmoved by the classic works of ancient and Renaissance art. What did impress him greatly was the experience of crossing the Alps. Not only did he produce some breathtaking views of mountain scenery, he also developed a preference for high viewpoints and panoramic scenes. The pictures for which he is most famous – peasant scenes full of incident – are far removed from the spirit of classical art.

Paradoxically, it was at the end of his career that Renaissance influence began to make itself felt in Bruegel's work. After he moved to Brussels in 1563, six years before his death, his work became simpler and grander, using fewer, but bigger and bolder figures. In this he seemed to have been influenced by Italian art, and perhaps specifically by the celebrated tapestry cartoons of Raphael (now in the Victoria and Albert Museum in London), which were then in Brussels, one of the most important centres of tapestry manufacture in Europe. Raphael's noble and grandiose works were then (and still are now) the greatest ensemble of High Renaissance art outside Italy and they had enormous influence. Although something of their spirit may be seen in Bruegel's late works, there are no specific borrowings. It is, indeed, in the work of minor artists of the period that the most obvious 'quotations' from ancient or Italian art are usually to be seen. Bruegel – together with Dürer, Cranach, Holbein and the other great artists of the Northern Renaissance – did not merely copy, but absorbed what he had seen and made it part of his own unique artistic personality.

Peasant Dance (c.1567)
(below) In the 16th century Bruegel earned the nickname, 'Peasant Bruegel' because of his many paintings on the theme. Here his picture of peasant revelry has a moral intention – the effects of excess are seen in the drunken quarrel on the far left.

Self-portrait: Dürer in 1500/Alte Pinakothek, Munich

ALBRECHT DÜRER

1471-1528

Albrecht Dürer was the greatest artist of the Northern Renaissance. He experimented in many media, and is as well-known for his delicate watercolours of animal and plant life as for the dramatic woodcuts and exquisite engravings on religious themes which brought him fame in his own time. His art is a blend of Northern and Southern traditions, profoundly influenced by the Venetian painting he saw during his visits to the city.

Dürer was an independent man, proud of his appearance and very sure of his talent. Intelligent and cultured, he mixed with humanists and scholars, while his patrons included the Holy Roman Emperor Maximilian I. A religious man throughout his life, in later years he became increasingly preoccupied with the advent of the Lutheran Reformation. He died in 1528 and was buried in his home town of Nuremberg.

The German Apelles

Enterprise and ambition helped Dürer to become an artist and printmaker of international renown. The humanist scholar Erasmus compared him with Apelles – the celebrated painter of antiquity.

Albrecht Dürer was born on 21 May 1471, in the south German city of Nuremberg. His father, a goldsmith from Hungary, had married Barbara Holper, his master's daughter, who went on to bear him eighteen children, of which Albrecht was the third.

As a child, Dürer attended a local Latin school, where he first met Willibald Pirckheimer, a young nobleman, who was to become a famous Humanist scholar and Dürer's lifelong friend and correspondent. For three years after leaving school Dürer followed custom and studied the goldsmith's trade in his father's workshop. Already he displayed signs of his wondrous artistic talent. In the memoir he wrote shortly before his death, Dürer recalled: 'My father took special pleasure in me, for he saw that I was eager to know how to do things and so he taught me the goldsmith's trade, and though I could do that work as neatly as you could wish, my heart was more for painting. I raised the whole question with my father, and he was far from happy about it, regretting all the time wasted, but just the same he gave in.'

At the age of fifteen Dürer was apprenticed to

Self-portrait
(right) In 1484, Dürer looked into a mirror and drew this self-portrait in silverpoint – using a silver stylus on specially coated paper. It is his earliest known work, executed at the age of 13, and already displays signs of the prodigious artistic talent which later brought him international renown.

Dürer's home town
(below) This painting shows Nuremberg in 1516, a prosperous city surrounded by forests. Dürer remained loyal to his birthplace, always returning to the city after his travels.

Archiv für Kunst und Geschichte

Albertina, Vienna

Archiv für Kunst und Geschichte

the Nuremberg painter Michael Wolgemut, a master of the old late medieval style. In 1490, after three years in Wolgemut's studio, Dürer set off on the traditional German 'bachelor's year', a period of wandering from city to city when life could be explored before settling down and accepting family responsibilities.

He travelled through much of what was then the Holy Roman Empire, and after two years arrived in Colmar in Alsace, now a German-speaking part of France. There he had hoped to meet Martin Schongauer, the greatest German engraver of the previous generation. Unfortunately, Schongauer had died only months before Dürer's arrival. Nonetheless, he stayed with the dead master's brother and no doubt learned from him some of the technical secrets he was later to use in his own work. Dürer also worked for publishers in Basel and Strasbourg, designing woodcut illustrations for Bibles and other books.

In 1493, his father arranged a marriage for him with the daughter of a local coppersmith, a girl named Agnes Frey. Dürer sent home a marvellous painted portrait of himself, then aged twenty two, which is the first independent self-portrait – painted only for the artist's personal satisfaction –

in the whole of European art. In it he appears a handsome if unusual looking youth, adorned in what today would be called fashionable, flamboyant clothes, proud of his long blond tresses and even prouder of his painterly skill.

Dürer returned to Nuremberg to be married in the spring of 1494. We know little of his wife's personality, though Pirckheimer complained in later years that she was 'nagging, shrewish, and greedy'. Within months of his marriage Dürer left his wife in Nuremberg and set off on his first journey to Italy, using money borrowed from Pirckheimer's family.

JOURNEY TO ITALY

There was plague in Nuremberg at the time and this may have been the young artist's motive for leaving the city. Whatever the reason, there can be little doubt that Dürer was powerfully attracted by what he must have heard, during his earlier travels, of the feats of the new Italian masters of painting and drawing. German artists, he said, were 'unconscious as a wild, uncut tree', whereas the Italians had 'rediscovered two hundred years ago the art revered by the Greeks and Romans'.

There were no carriage facilities for long-distance travel at that time and the journey over the Alps on horseback must have been a perilous one. On his way Dürer recorded his impression of the mountain scenery in a series of brilliant watercolours. In Pavia he visited Pirckheimer, who was completing his studies at the great university there, and through him Dürer came to know of the work of the Italian Humanists, whose scientific curiosity and independence of mind

Photo Hinz

Beloved mother
(below) Dürer drew this charcoal portrait of his mother shortly before her death in 1514. He said he loved her more than anyone else in the world.

Albrecht the elder
(below) This portrait of Dürer's father shows him saying the rosary. Dürer wrote: 'My father was a man of very few words and deeply pious.'

Centre for books
(above) The city of Basel was a European centre for publishing illustrated books. Dürer worked here in 1492 during his 'bachelor's year'.

Key Dates

1471 born in Nuremberg

1490 sets out on his 'bachelor's year'

1494 marries Agnes Frey; travels to Italy

1496 first meeting with Frederick the Wise

1498 publishes *The Apocalypse of St John*

1502 father dies

1505 travels to Venice

1512 employed by Emperor Maximilian I

1514 death of mother; engraves *Melencolia I*

1520 travels to the Netherlands

1526 presents *The Four Apostles* to the city of Nuremberg

1528 dies in Nuremberg

Giraudon

Scala

Kupferstichkabinett, Berlin

Uffizi, Florence

appealed to him strongly.

The highlight of his journey was Venice. With his unquenchable thirst for knowledge and his customary diligence, Dürer set himself to learn all that contemporary Italian masters could teach him. He studied the science of perspective and the portrayal of the nude. He copied the works of Mantegna and other engravers, and argued over the various theories of art with the sociable circle of Venetian painters.

When he returned home the following year he brought with him the rudiments of the Italian Renaissance and the ambition to transplant them to his native northern soil. He made a living from his woodcuts and engravings, often single sheet designs which his wife and mother would hawk in the public markets and fairs, and which were carried all over Europe by the town's travelling merchants.

These were tumultuous years in central Europe. Many preachers foretold the world would end in the year 1500. These feelings of doom were brilliantly summed up in Dürer's illustrations to *The Apocalypse of St. John* (1498), his first

Kupferstichkabinett, Berlin

masterwork. Although they were printed with a text at the famous press of his godfather, Anton Koberger, in Nuremberg, Dürer insisted that his own name appear as the publisher. This was part of his life-long campaign to raise the status of the artist in northern Europe and to secure recognition for his own genius. Two years later he painted another self-portrait (p.11), facing the viewer directly in a pose deliberately reminiscent of Christ. The portrait displays the pride and self-consciousness of a man who was by then well aware of his own unique artistic destiny.

In the years that followed, Dürer slowly digested the lessons of his Italian journey and produced a remarkable variety of work. Some

A mountain scene
(above) In 1495, travelling back from Venice, Dürer made sketches and watercolours of the scenery along the way. This is Wehlsch Pirg – a view of the South Tyrol mountains to the east of Trent.

A life-long friend
(left) Dürer sketched this charcoal portrait of Willibald Pirckheimer, his best friend since childhood, in 1503. The son of wealthy parents Pirckheimer was a humanist and poet who introduced Dürer to the Greek and Latin classics.

An eye for detail
(right) On his first visit to Venice in 1495, Dürer made this detailed watercolour sketch of a crab he saw in a fish market. He was fascinated by the natural world, and by unusual objects – shellfish would not have been a common sight in Nuremberg.

commissions for painting came in from burghers and aristocrats, including the powerful Elector of Saxony, Frederick the Wise. But it was his woodcuts and increasingly his engravings on copperplate which spread his fame and earned him the independence he so desperately craved.

In the late summer of 1505 Dürer headed south once again. He had received a commission to paint an altarpiece for the wealthy association of German merchants in Venice. This time he settled in the great island city for more than a year. By then his engravings were well-known in Italy and tributes flowed from other artists as well as from such eminent men as the Doge and Patriarch of Venice, both of whom visited his studio. Dürer was determined to show the Venetians that he was not only a clever draughtsman but also a master of colour and paint equal to the enigmatic Giorgione, whose haunting images were then causing a tremendous stir. It was, however, the aged Giovanni Bellini, the grand master of the previous generation, whose work Dürer most admired. When the 80-year-old Bellini visited Dürer in his

Boymans-Van Beunigen, Rotterdam

studio and praised his work, it was a proud moment for the young German artist, then 35 years of age.

Dürer enjoyed Venetian life, the company of other artists, the food and wine and the beauty of the city. Most of all he enjoyed the respect accorded by the Italians to their artists, in sharp contrast to the penny-pinching ways of the German burghers. 'How I shall shiver for the sun,' he wrote, contemplating his return, 'Here I am a gentleman, at home a parasite'. However, when Venice offered him two hundred ducats to remain in its service for a year, he refused, and returned home in January 1507.

Back in Nuremberg, there were only few opportunities for any of the large-scale public commissions with which his Italian rivals made their reputations. Increasingly he abandoned painting and concentrated on graphic work. His popularity grew and in 1509 he was at last able to purchase outright the house his family had rented for some years.

After 1512 he was favoured by the Holy Roman Emperor Maximilian I. Dürer decorated a prayer

Ashmolean Museum, Oxford

Bildarchiv Preussischer Kulturbesitz

Staatliche Museen, Berlin

Marriage of Convenience

While he was enjoying his traditional 'bachelor's year' of travel, Dürer's parents – as was the custom – arranged his marriage to a local girl called Agnes Frey. Dürer returned home for the wedding but left for Italy, alone, almost immediately after. This was to be the pattern for the rest of his married life. They had no children and Agnes usually had to stay out of the way and eat in the kitchen with the servants when her husband had important visitors. But it should be remembered that marriage in those days was regarded more as a business contract than an emotional one.

New home
(below) By 1509, Dürer was doing sufficiently well to be able to buy this impressive house in Nuremberg's Siztelgasse. He moved with his wife and his mother and stayed there until he died.

Patron of the arts
(above) Frederick the Wise, Elector of Saxony and patron of the arts, was to become Dürer's first benefactor and remain so throughout his life. He met Dürer on a visit to Nuremberg in 1496 and commissioned this portrait, painted in tempera on linen.

Albertina, Vienna

Bildagentur Mauritius

Young wife
(above) Agnes Frey was 15 when she married Dürer in 1494. Pirckheimer, his friend, did not like her and called her 'nagging, jealous, shrewish'.

POTENTISSIMVS MAXIMVS ET INVICTISSIMVS CÆSAR MAXIMILIANVS
QVI CVNCTOS SVI TEMPORIS REGES ET PRINCIPES IVSTICIA PRVDENCIA
MAGNANIMITATE LIBERALITATE PRÆCIPVE VERO BELLICA LAVDE ET
ANIMI FORTITVDINE SVPERAVIT NATVS EST ANNO SALVTIS HVMANÆ
M CCCC LIX DIE MARCII IX VIXIT ANNOS LIX MENSES IX DIES XXV
DECESSIT VERO ANNO M D XIX MENSIS IANVARII DIE XII QVEM DEVS
OPT MAX IN NVMERVM VIVENCIVM REFERRE VELIT

Kunsthistorisches Museum, Vienna

The Emperor's favour
*(above) The Holy Roman
Emperor, Maximilian I,
employed Dürer from
1512 and in 1515 awarded
him a pension of 100
florins a year. This
portrait was painted after
Maximilian's death in
1519. He holds a
pomegranate – his own
personal symbol of
immortality.*

book for him, and collaborated on the creation of
the *Triumphal Arch*, an enormous composition in
the shape of an arch, made up of hundreds of
separate woodcuts. In 1513 Dürer was made an
honorary citizen of the Great Council of
Nuremberg, an unprecedented honour for an
artist working north of the Alps, and in 1515 the
Emperor granted him an annuity of one hundred
florins for the rest of his life.

DIFFICULT YEARS

Despite this public success, these were difficult
years for Dürer. Though his income was relatively
high, his expenses quickly offset it. He spent and
loaned money freely, filling his house with strange
and precious objects of all kinds. His mother's
death in 1514 affected him deeply, and he
underwent an artistic and spiritual crisis which is
reflected in his engraving *Melencolia I* (p.33). He
was still obsessed with the grandeur of the Italian
achievements and in particular with the ideals of
beauty and harmony which always seemed to
elude him.

In 1517 Martin Luther made his first great attack
on corruption in the Church, thus beginning the
upheaval in European religious life that came to be
known as the Reformation. Dürer read avidly
Luther's writings which were passed to him by
Reformers such as Philip Melanchthon, a

Netherlands Journey

While the Holy Roman Emperor Maximilian I
was alive Dürer received an annuity of 100 florins,
to be paid by the Nuremberg city treasury. But
when the Emperor died in January 1519, the
city council said the contract was no longer
binding and refused to pay. Dürer decided to
travel to the Netherlands to petition the new
Emperor. It was to be an extremely successful
trip, and he was welcomed and fêted as an
honoured artist by every town along the way.

Humanist scholar who, like Dürer himself, tried to
bridge the gap between the new learning from
Italy and the new piety from Germany. Luther's
teachings appear to have brought Dürer some
relief from his inner turmoil.

When Emperor Maximilian I died in 1519, the
Nuremberg Council stopped Dürer's life pension,
prompting his lengthy journey to the Netherlands
to meet the new Emperor and petition for the
renewal of his annuity. He left Nuremberg in 1520,
accompanied by his wife and maidservant. With
him he took engravings and woodcuts, with which
he was able to pay his way throughout his trip. He
kept a detailed journal in which he recorded all his
expenses and everything he saw or heard, as well
as sketchbooks which he filled with drawings.
Everywhere he was received by the rich and
mighty and fêted as the greatest German artist of
his time. For Dürer it was the fulfilment of his
longstanding dream of raising the public status of
the artist.

Along his route Dürer made it his business to
see the notable works of art and the important
artists in each town. He made a difficult excursion
to Zeeland in the wild north of the country to see
and draw a whale that had been beached there, but
by the time he arrived the creature had already
returned to the sea. While in Zeeland, he caught
some kind of fever which was to weaken him for
much of the rest of his life. In Aachen he witnessed

the coronation of the new Emperor, Charles V, and when the court moved to Cologne his annuity was confirmed. He painted many portraits and sold many prints but so indulged his love of collecting – including such objects as tortoise-shells, parrots, coral, conch shells and ivory – that overall he made a financial loss on the trip.

Dürer was in Antwerp when news arrived of Luther's arrest. He and his wife hurried home, possibly in fear of attack by pro-Catholic elements in Antwerp. They arrived in Nuremberg in August 1521, to find the city in turmoil. Friends and pupils of Dürer's had been banished for heretical ideas. In the surrounding countryside discontent was mounting which would eventually explode in the Peasants' War of 1525. Dürer, though careful to remain on the right side of the authorities, none-theless expressed some sympathy for the new movements.

In his last great painting, *The Four Apostles*, his deep religious feeling was perfectly combined with his love of Venetian art. He made a gift of the painting to the Council of Nuremberg in 1526, carefully inscribing it with this warning: 'All worldly rulers in these dangerous times should pay heed lest they follow human misguidance instead of the word of God. For God will have nothing added to his word nor taken away from it.'

A TIME FOR WRITING

Dürer concentrated much of his strength in his last years on his writings. He published works on proportion, perspective, and fortification and composed his family chronicle and his memoirs. He also started, but did not live to finish, a work of advice for young artists. His old friend Pirckheimer lamented his deteriorating condition: 'He was withered like a bundle of straw and could never be a happy man or mingle with people'. On 6 April 1528, at the age of 57, in his home city of Nuremberg, Dürer died of the fever he had first contracted in Zeeland. He was mourned by Melanchthon who described him as a 'wise man whose artistic talents, eminent as they were, were still the least of his virtues'.

The city of Aachen
(left) Charles V, in the tradition of earlier Holy Roman Emperors, was crowned in the ancient city of Aachen. Dürer arrived there in time for the coronation in October 1520, hoping to press his petition after the ceremony.

The coronation
(above) Charles' coronation was a splendid affair, described by Dürer as 'more magnificent than anything that those who live in our parts have ever seen' – too magnificent, in fact, for Dürer to have his petition heard.

Lauros-Giraudon

Kunsthistorisches Museum, Vienna

Dürer's dream vision
(above) In the summer of 1525, Dürer had a vivid nightmare about the end of the world. He wrote: 'When I got up in the morning I painted it above, just as I had seen it'.

A visit to Antwerp
(right) Dürer and his wife arrived in Antwerp in 1520, on their way to see the Emperor. This ink drawing of the harbour is one of many Dürer made during his journey to the Netherlands.

Albertina, Vienna

The Engraver's Art

Dürer became the first exponent of the Renaissance north of the Alps, but it was his exceptionally fine prints rather than his paintings which established his reputation as a great artist.

'Only a dried-up mind has no confidence in itself to find its way to something further, and so drags on in the same old path content to imitate others and without the gumption to think ahead for itself.' So wrote Albrecht Dürer, and his own work stands as the best illustration of the unquenchable curiosity and probing spirit he admired. This spirit took him from the Nuremberg goldsmith's workshop of his father, steeped in medieval tradition, to the pinnacle of achievement as the first German master of the Renaissance.

THE ITALIAN INFLUENCE

Dürer's art was rooted deeply in the Northern tradition, and shaped by his visits to Italy and his contact with the Renaissance. In his first great work, the illustrations to *The Apocalypse*, published in 1498 shortly after his return from Italy, Dürer showed both what made him a new kind of artist north of the Alps and what still linked him to the old ways. These terrifying visions of the end of the world were topical for the people of Dürer's time. Many of them believed the year 1500 would usher in the Last Judgement, and the war, disease and turmoil of the era found expression in Dürer's violent, vibrant images.

The woodcut technique Dürer used had been popular in Germany for some time, but in Dürer's

Gift of M and P.J. Sachs

The Four Horsemen/Fogg Art Museum, Harvard

Visions of The Apocalypse (1498)
(left) Dürer's first masterwork includes this powerful image of doom. The Four Horsemen – Death, Famine, Pestilence and War – trample everything in their path.

The Heron (1502-3)
(below, left) One of many watercolours of birds, animals and plants, this painting of a heron shows Dürer's fascination with the natural world and his painstaking attention to minute detail.

Hands of an Apostle (1508)
(below) This highly finished brush drawing is one of several preliminary studies for an altarpiece commissioned by the wealthy Frankfurt merchant Jacob Heller.

Bildarchiv Preussischer Kulturbesitz

Kupferstichkabinett, Berlin

Albertina, Vienna

Kunsthistorisches Museum, Vienna

Portraits of the later years

(below) Dürer's study of the human body culminated in the outstanding portraits of his last years. In this portrait of Jacob Muffel, the features are sculpturally modelled with a softness lacking in earlier works.

Staatliche Museen, Berlin

Virgin and Child (1512)
(above) Also known as Virgin with the Pear, this oil painting of the Madonna is one of many devotional pictures which Dürer painted during his lifetime. Executed after his second visit to Venice, the painting is a mixture of the Northern and Southern traditions. The Italian influence is evident in the vibrant colours and classical figures of mother and child, while the Virgin's dress is essentially Northern in character.

hands it reached new heights of expressiveness. He drew his designs directly on soft wood and they were then chiselled out by highly trained craftsmen. The remaining, raised parts of the block would be inked and then printed on paper.

In these prints Dürer made use of the Italian techniques of drawing the figure – especially the short 'modelling' lines which give it its roundness – and his angels, devils and humans have a three-dimensional thrust hitherto unseen in the woodcut. He also borrowed Italian discoveries in perspective – the ability to present a given space in consistent depth – to set his visionary drama in a world understandable to ordinary human beings.

However, in many respects *The Apocalypse* woodcuts are still rooted in Dürer's native traditions and could never be mistaken for Italian work. The tormented faces, the jostling crowds, the hideous demons are all portrayed with a distinctive angular, elaborate line that is entirely Dürer's own. He had learned from the Italians but used that learning to express a passionate and personal religious feeling.

This mixture of styles can also be seen in Dürer's many paintings, woodcuts and engravings of other episodes from the New Testament – he rarely chose subjects from the Old. In *The Adoration of the Magi* (pp.28-9) the vibrant colours, the geometric structure of the composition and the use of classical architecture are all evidence of the influence of Bellini and Leonardo. At the same time the figures and the landscape in the background are distinctly Northern in character.

PERFECT PROPORTIONS

Increasingly, for Dürer, the human being was the central concern of art, and the human figure the basis of that concern. He studied the nude ceaselessly. During his first visit to Venice he copied the classical nudes of the Italian artists and engravers Antonio Pollaiuolo and Mantegna, and in his drawings, paintings and his fine engraving *The Fall of Man* (p.20), he sought a formula for representing the body, a guideline for the perfect proportion of head, legs, torso and arms. Though

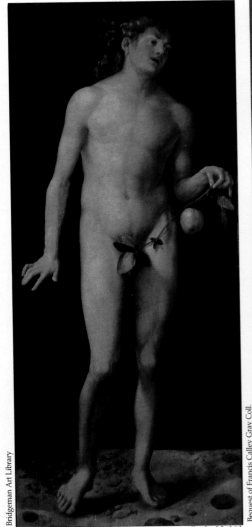

Prado, Madrid

Fogg Art Museum, Harvard

Adam (1507)
*(above) One of the first
life-size nudes in the
history of German
painting, this work was
painted after Dürer's
second visit to Italy. The
continuous contours of the
body and the soft
modelling of the flesh
replace the earlier sharply
defined, muscular figures
in* The Fall of Man.

The Fall of Man (1504)
*(above right) This
exquisite engraving is a
landmark in Dürer's
search for the perfect form.
The graceful, classical
figures of Adam and Eve
are set against a dense
forest full of Northern,
iconographic significance.*

he came to realize that there were many such
formulas, and no one reliable measure of beauty,
these efforts enlarged the scope of his work and
helped him to achieve on the small scale of the
woodcut or engraving the kind of grandeur Italian
artists achieved in frescoes or paintings.

A striking feature of Dürer's paintings and
engravings is his mastery of minute detail. He
drew endless studies of hands, heads, household
objects, plants and animals, and incorporated the
results of his observations with painstaking care in
his major works. 'The tiniest detail should be done
skilfully and as well as possible,' he said, 'nor
should the slightest wrinkles and puckers be
omitted.' His fine sympathetic portraits of
Humanists and burghers alike bear witness to this
belief, as do his magnificently detailed drawings of
animals such as the famous *Hare* (p.26). Like
Leonardo, he was fascinated by the natural world,
but whereas his Italian contemporary was
obsessed by particular subjects, Dürer drew and
painted anything which caught his eye. He
believed that 'truly art is contained within nature
and he who can seize it has got it'. His shimmering
watercolour sketches of mountain scenery –

unique in their day – show his truth to nature at its
most acute.

Some of Dürer's greatest works are his
copperplate engravings. This technique, which
derived from a combination of woodcut printing
and ornamental engraving on silver and gold was
peculiarly suited to him, given his training as a
goldsmith. Dürer himself cut the design on to a
copper plate using a metal burin, like a delicate
chisel, which required tremendous patience,
keeness of eye, and steadiness of hand. The
printers would then rub ink into the cut-out
grooves and press the plate on to damp paper.

THE TRIUMPH OF LINE

Dürer's engravings display an amazing variety of
tones and textures and subtle gradations of light
and shade. They are not only the most technically
accomplished engravings ever produced, they also
express a range of feeling never before seen on
such a small scale. His skill and originality reach
unparalleled heights in three large and personal
engravings *The Knight, Death and the Devil* (p.32),
Melencolia I (p.33) and *St Jerome in his Study*.

20

Dürer's unflagging appetite for experiment led him to develop a facility in many media. He was one of the first artists to try the new process of copperplate etching, which involved drawing the design on a wax ground melted over the surface of the plate and immersing it in acid to etch out the lines. He explored the complex realms of art theory in pursuit of knowledge, publishing his findings in treatises on measurement and human proportions, and made detailed notes of nature's humblest phenomena. Yet this many-sided activity was always an expression of his own individuality, that of a religious man, deeply moved by the teachings of Martin Luther, who was nevertheless also a man of science, fascinated by the natural world.

Dürer's art spanned two eras, the medieval and the Renaissance, and two worlds of feeling, the classical Italian and the spiritual Northern. In his own day this brought him unprecedented recognition and praise. He himself wrote, in his fiercely proud spirit of self-examination: 'God often gives the ability to learn and the insight to make something good to one man the like of whom nobody is found in his own days, and nobody comes after him very soon.'

Northern symbolism
The branch represents the tree of life and the parrot symbolizes wisdom.

TRADEMARKS

The Skilful Use of Line

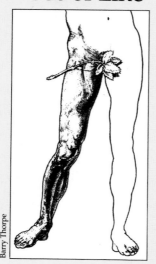

Dürer lightly incised the outline of the engraving before filling in detail with delicate lines to give shading and texture.

COMPARISONS

Naturalist Paintings

Dürer's delicate watercolours of animals and plants were unusual in their time, although his fascination with the natural world was shared by his Italian contemporary Leonardo, who made detailed drawings of plant life. Other parallels include the formal studies found in illuminated manuscripts of the period, such as *The Hours of Anne of Brittany* by the French painter Jean Bourdichon: these botanical paintings were instructional as well as decorative. In the 18th century the British artist George Stubbs became celebrated for his paintings of horses and other animals, which, like the works of the Renaissance masters, were the result of acute observation and scientific study.

George Stubbs (1724-1806) **Green Monkey** *(left) Stubbs's painting is more than a faithful rendering of an exotic species – it captures the creature's timidity and readiness for flight.*

Jean Bourdichon (c.1457-1521) **The Hours of Anne of Brittany** *(right) This chamomile is one of more than 50 paintings of flowers, fruit and insects which adorn the manuscript, completed in 1508.*

Walker Art Gallery, Liverpool

THE MAKING OF A MASTERPIECE

The Feast of the Rose Garlands

Dürer began this painting in February 1506, soon after his arrival in Venice. It was commissioned by a group of German merchants for a chapel in San Bartolommeo, the German national church near the German merchants' centre, the Fondaco dei Tedeschi. The subject chosen was a *Rosenkranzbild*, a traditional picture of the Madonna and child showing the rite of the rosary. The distribution of the rose garlands – which symbolize the rosary – to laymen and clergy, men and women, rich and poor, illustrates the idea of the universal brotherhood of Christianity. The monumentality of the painting, with its geometric symmetry and vivid colouring, shows the influence of Venetian art, although the landscape and crowded figures are typically Northern. Dürer was particularly pleased with this work, which proved his ability as a painter.

Narodni Galerie, Prague

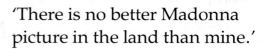

'There is no better Madonna picture in the land than mine.'

Albrecht Dürer 1506

A tribute to Bellini
(above) This seated angel was copied from Bellini's altarpiece for San Zaccaria, completed shortly before Dürer's arrival in Venice. Its inclusion is a tribute to an artist Dürer admired.

Self-portrait of the artist
(right) Dürer included his own self-portrait on the right of the painting. The scroll he holds bears an inscription in Latin claiming the picture was completed in five months.

People in the painting

(right) The strong characterization of figures in the painting suggest that many are portraits. Some can be identified.

A. Pope Julius II
B. Cardinal Grimani
C. St Dominic
D. Emperor Maximilian I
E. Girolamo Tedesco
F. Dürer
G. Venetian ecclesiastics
H. German merchants and Venetian officials of the Fondaco dei Tedeschi.

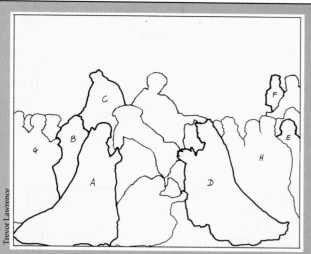

Trevor Lawrence

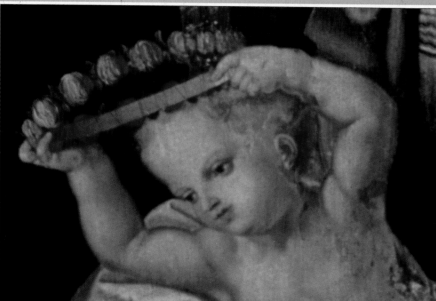

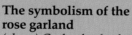

Albertina, Vienna

The pope's robes

(above) This delicate preparatory study of the pope's robes was transplanted almost directly to the finished oil painting.

Portrait of an architect

(below) Girolamo Tedesco was a German architect who was supervising the rebuilding of the Fondaco dei Tedeschi, damaged by fire in 1505.

The symbolism of the rose garland

(above) Garlands of red roses represent the Our Fathers of the rosary and the Sorrowful Mysteries of the Passion. White roses symbolize the Hail Marys and the Joyful Mysteries of the Virgin.

Alpine landscape

(left) Watercolours such as this view of Arco, made on Dürer's return from Venice in 1495, provided the basis for the rocky Alpine landscape in the background of the painting.

Reunion des Musées Nationaux

Louvre, Paris

Kupferstichkabinett, Berlin

Gallery

Dürer was still in his twenties when he established himself as the leading artist in his native city of Nuremberg. His self-portrait, painted when he was 27, clearly conveys his self-confidence and pride in his abilities. His skill as a portraitist gained him numerous commissions from Nuremberg's leading citizens, but his visual curiosity led

Artothek

Self-portrait 1498
20½″ × 16¼″
Prado, Madrid

Dürer was obviously proud of his appearance and painted several self-portraits. In this one he is elegantly dressed in the height of fashion. He saw himself as a cultured gentleman rather than as a humble artisan, which had been the traditional status of artists.

him to lavish as much attention on humble subjects such as A Hare as on more traditional – and lucrative – themes.

Dürer's two visits to Italy profoundly affected his art. In such ambitious works as The Adoration of the Magi and The Festival of the Rose Garlands he rivalled the great Italian painters in richness of colouring, and in The Four Apostles he matched the heroic and monumental grandeur of the masters of the High Renaissance.

It was on his prints that Dürer's international reputation was based: engravings such as The Knight, Death and the Devil and Melencolia I were regarded with a new kind of seriousness.

Lauros-Giraudon

Portrait of Elsbeth Tucher 1499
11″ × 8¾″
Gemäldegalerie, Kassel

The Tuchers were one of the leading families of Nuremberg. There was probably originally a companion portrait of Elsbeth's husband, showing him facing her, as Dürer painted another married couple from the family in this format.

A Hare 1502
9¾″ × 8¾″ Albertina, Vienna

*This marvellously naturalistic animal study is justifiably one of
Dürer's most popular works. It is painted in watercolour and gouache
(opaque water-colour, now often called poster-colour). Dürer was a
born craftsman and complete master of every technique to which he
turned his hand.*

The Large Piece of Turf 1503
16¼″ × 12½″ Albertina, Vienna

Dürer looked at the natural world with acute powers of observation. This water-colour is accurate down to the last detail (all the plants can be identified), but it rises far above mere botanical illustration. Dürer did a similar but smaller watercolour, which is known as The Little Piece of Turf *to distinguish it from this one.*

The Adoration of the Magi 1504
38½" × 44" Uffizi, Florence

*This splendid altarpiece was commissioned by Frederick
the Wise, Elector of Saxony. It was painted between
Dürer's two visits to Italy and shows a typical fusing of
Italian and Northern elements. The precision of line and
love of ornament are characteristically Northern, but the
glowing light and various distinctive details show the
influence of the South. In particular, the ruinous
architectural setting with the prancing horse in the
background recalls Leonardo da Vinci's famous
treatment of the subject, which is now also in the Uffizi.*

Scala

The Feast of the Rose Garlands 1506
63¾″ × 76½″ National Gallery, Prague

Dürer painted this picture in Venice during his second trip to Italy. It is full of symbolic detail, but in essence it represents the idea of a universal brotherhood of Christianity. The picture was a great success and in its wake Dürer was offered, but declined, a position as one of Venice's official painters.

The Adoration of the Trinity 1511
53¼″ × 48½″ Kunsthistorisches Museum, Vienna

*This altarpiece was commissioned by Mattheus Landauer, a rich
Nuremberg merchant, for a chapel dedicated to the Trinity and All
Saints. A host of figures, heavenly and earthly, adore the Trinity
(Father, Son and Holy Ghost – represented by the dove) and in the
bottom right-hand corner Dürer has included a self-portrait.*

The Knight, Death and the Devil 1513
9½″ × 7½″ Fogg Art Museum, Cambridge, Massachusetts

*This magnificent engraving shows the prodigious skill with which
Dürer rivalled the richness and textures of painting purely through
black lines. The knight is a personification of Christian faith, his
steadfastness taking him past the powers of darkness. The horse recalls
Verrocchio's Colleoni Monument, which Dürer saw in Venice.*

Melencolia I 1514
9½" × 7½" Fogg Art Museum, Cambridge, Massachusetts

*Melancholy was the daughter of Saturn and symbolized intellectual,
introspective qualities. Here she sits in perplexed contemplation,
contrasting with the child on the millstone, who is happily –
unthinkingly – active. When thought is not directed to practical ends it
leads to the first stage of melancholy – Melencolia I.*

Artothek

The Four Apostles 1526
Each panel 84¾″ × 30″
Alte Pinakothek, Munich

*These panels form Dürer's last
great masterpiece in painting,
memorably combining Northern
precision of detail with Italian
amplitude of form. St John and
St Peter are shown on the left, St
Paul and St Mark on the right.
The panels may have originally
been conceived as wings of a
triptych, but Dürer himself
presented them to the city of
Nuremberg as a pair.*

The City of Nuremberg

Nuremberg was a microcosm of 15th-century cultural life. The arts, learning and printing flourished there, fostered by the city's enlightened climate and commercial prosperity.

Archiv für Kunst und Geschichte

An attractive city
(left) This woodcut, from the famous Nuremberg Chronicle, *shows the walled city of Nuremberg in 1492. The Kaiserburg (imperial castle) sits imposingly on the crown of the hill, looking down over a sea of red-roofed houses. The spires of the two medieval churches of St Lorenz and St Sebald are clearly visible.*

Dürer's Nuremberg was one of the liveliest, most exciting cities in 15th-century Europe. Referred to variously by contemporaries as the 'Florence of the North' and as a 'German Athens', it was a major cultural, commercial and artistic centre at the hub of the Holy Roman Empire. The successes of its citizens in all spheres of life were impressive, and were crowned by the achievements of Dürer himself, whose fame was to stretch far beyond the city boundaries.

Germany in the 15th century was composed of various principalities, dukedoms, bishoprics and cities which were loosely grouped under the authority of the Holy Roman Empire of the German nation. By Dürer's time, the cities were probably the most powerful section of the Empire, enjoying considerable prosperity and stable government. This was especially true of the 65 or so Imperial cities, which were then largely independent, except for a number of stipulated obligations to the emperor such as tax payments,

hospitality and allegiance. In return, the emperor guaranteed the citizens peace, and granted them certain specific privileges.

Imperial cities such as Ulm, Strasbourg, Augsburg and Cologne were major European centres during this period but one of the most important of all was Nuremberg. The esteem in which this city was held was reflected in the fact that as well as being a venue of Imperial Diets or parliaments it was the city in which the Imperial regalia and relics were housed from 1423.

Visually, Nuremberg must have been an extremely attractive city. Built on the river Pegnitz, it was surrounded by woods and the view of the walled city was dominated by the grand imperial castle, set on a hill overlooking the red-roofed houses. The triple encircling walls had four gates and 128 towers. Other landmarks were the impressive churches of St Lorenz and St Sebald.

Living conditions in Nuremberg, however, must have been fairly cramped. At the time of

A leading artist
(right) Michael Wolgemut, now remembered chiefly as Dürer's master, was the principal painter of 15th-century Nuremberg. He ran an industrious workshop and, in the second half of his career, devoted a great deal of his energies to book illustration, collaborating closely with the city's printers. It was Wolgemut who supplied the delightful woodcuts for the Nuremberg Chronicle.

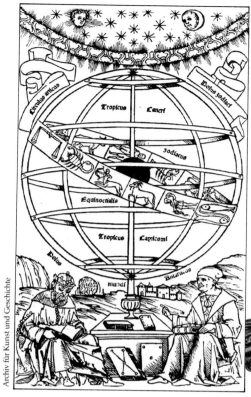

Dürer's birth the population was about 40,000. Within the city walls, which were only about 8,000 paces in circumference, there were over five hundred streets, and thousands of public and private buildings.

The city's government was in the hands of its Council which was made up of 42 men, drawn largely from the urban patriciate. The Council ruled absolutely and very successfully, showing continual concern for the well-being of the citizens. Almost uniquely among Imperial cities, Nuremberg was renowned for its stability and freedom from internal trouble or strife of any sort, and this was mostly because the Council simply did not allow it to happen.

A CENTRE OF COMMERCE

International comings and goings were an accepted way of life in Nuremberg and resulted from the city's success as the major business centre of south Germany. All types of trades and crafts were represented in the city – furriers, belt-makers, cloth-makers, armourers and paper-makers. The silver- and goldsmiths were particularly prominent and many of Germany's finest artists began their careers in these crafts. Dürer himself was apprenticed as a goldsmith, and both his father and grandfather were masters of the craft.

The prosperity generated by Nuremberg's commercial successes meant that the standard of living was generally very high for almost all of its citizens, and they lived comfortably according to their own social standing. This is proved by the fact that nearly every family had their own house, which also served as a workplace. The people dressed well, and ate well – indeed, it was normal for a citizen of Nuremberg to have at least one meat dish a day. The most popular drink was beer which was brewed locally.

However, the well-ordered city of Nuremberg

A haven for scholars
(above) As a centre of learning, Nuremberg attracted some of the greatest scholars in Europe. The famous astronomer and mathematician, Johann Müller, settled there in 1471, established the first European observatory and wrote a book on Ptolemaic astronomy.

Prosperous citizens
(above right) Dürer's costume drawing shows a Nuremberg woman dressed to go dancing. In general, the citizens of Nuremberg were well-dressed and well-fed, whatever their social standing. Indeed, most families owned their own homes, which doubled as workplaces.

Printmaking
(below) Nuremberg drew on its commercial and artistic expertise for one of its most successful business ventures – printmaking. In the latter half of the 15th century, 'blockbooks' were very popular. For these the illustration and text were both printed from the woodblock.

Albrecht Dürer/Wolgemut/German National Museum, Nürnberg

Gutenberg's Bible
(below) The great predecessor of the Nuremberg Chronicle, Gutenberg's Bible *(c.1455) was deliberately designed to look like a hand-illuminated manuscript and had no printed illustrations.*

was not only renowned for its commercial and material successes. Throughout Dürer's lifetime it was also famous as a centre of learning, despite the fact that it had no university. Largely due to its trade links with Italy, Nuremberg had been very much influenced by the southern Renaissance and had become one of the major centres of humanism in Germany. Scholars were drawn to Nuremberg from all over Europe, and the city also had its own humanist 'society', of which a prominent member was Willibald Pirckheimer, a close friend of Dürer. The mathematician, Johann Müller – who further developed trigonometry – settled in Nuremberg in 1471, because here, as he said he could easily 'keep in touch with the learned of all countries . . .'

FLOWERING OF THE ARTS

The presence of humanism in the city, combined with its affluence, provided a flourishing climate for art in the late 15th century. The prosperity of the citizens encouraged them to patronize the local painters and sculptors, and the city churches, in particular, were filled with artistic decorations donated by parishioners. In fact the city's artistic life was at its peak between 1490 and 1525, the very period in which Dürer came to prominence. One of the most famous of these artists was Michael Wolgemut, now remembered chiefly as Dürer's teacher. During the last third of the 15th century he was Nuremberg's principal painter, printmaker and stained-glass designer. He became an independent master in 1473, and set up one of the largest workshops in the city.

The thriving artistic profession in 15th-century Nuremberg was very closely connected to the city's commercial skills. The two areas complemented each other, and many men were active in both fields. These links between trade and

Archiv für Kunst und Geschichte

Anton Koberger
(left) Koberger was Dürer's godfather and established Nuremberg's printing reputation.

A grandiose project
(right) One of the curiosities of early printing was the Triumphal Arch of Maximilian *(1515) – an 11 by 10 foot arch printed from 192 separate blocks. Dürer, who was by now Nuremberg's most famous artist, was made designer-in-chief of the project. He also worked on the accompanying* Triumphal Procession, *producing two woodcuts showing Maximilian's wedding chariot.*

Archiv für Kunst und Geschichte

Inside a 15th-century printing room
(below) In the background, apprentices are choosing the matrices (engraved letter blocks) to insert into the form. The printer in the left foreground has just removed a new printed sheet. His associate inks the press bed to receive another sheet.

The Creation
(right) This coloured woodcut by Wolgemut is one of over 650 woodcuts decorating the massive **Nuremberg Chronicle,** *one of the city's greatest ventures. It attempts to tell in words and pictures the history of life from the Creation to 1493, the year of publication.*

culture were nowhere more evident than in one of the city's most modern and most successful business ventures – the establishment of printing. Nuremberg was famous among the Imperial cities for its printmaking and this reputation was earned largely by the work of one man, Anton Koberger, Dürer's godfather. In 1470, only a decade after printing first appeared in the city, Koberger set up his own press and combined printing, publishing and bookselling in his business. He was, by any standards, phenomenally successful.

Koberger's success coincided with dramatic improvements in paper manufacture which resulted in an explosion of printed material. Between the years 1473 and 1513, Koberger's press produced more than 200 titles. At its height, his workshop had more than 24 presses, with over one hundred compositors, proof-readers, illuminators and binders. He set up European-wide trade links, and even had his own agency in Paris. Koberger was the first publisher to climb the social scale as a result of his commercial success, and even became a member of the city's most elite group, the Council. The links between trade and

art in Nuremberg are highlighted by the fact that Koberger allowed his godson, Albrecht Dürer, to use his presses and types for the *Apocalypse* series.

One of Koberger's publications perfectly demonstrates Nuremberg's dominance in all spheres of German life during the Renaissance. This was the production, in 1493, of the *Nuremberg Chronicle,* the first great illustrated book, which told the world's history from the Creation to 1493.

The Chronicle was written by a prominent local humanist, Hartmann Schedel, who collaborated with the printer Koberger and the artist Wolgemut to produce what is probably the most famous 15th-century publication after Gutenberg's Bible. Published in both Latin and German, the *Nuremberg Chronicle* is famous today for its woodcut illustrations. These were done in Wolgemut's workshop, and some were probably the work of his apprentice, Dürer. The *Nuremberg Chronicle* – the fruit of the city's intellectual, commercial and artistic endeavours – leaves us with a fitting and lasting testimony to the pre-eminence of the Imperial city of Nuremberg in Dürer's lifetime.

A Year in the Life 1521

The year started with the excommunication of Martin Luther from the Church of Rome. The Lutheran faction spread through Germany, a war was brewing with nearby France and English support was being sought by both sides. By autumn, England and Germany had formed a powerful alliance against the French.

On 3 January 1521, a papal bull of excommunication was issued against the Augustinian monk and ardent church reformer, Martin Luther. It was a little over three years since Luther had nailed a placard to the door of the castle church at Wittenberg in Germany on which he had written his '95 Theses' attacking the Catholic system of Indulgences, and particularly their 'sale' to help fund the rebuilding of St Peter's in Rome. Luther's original aim was simply to purify the Catholic church and return to the fundamental truths of Christianity. But by 1521 his name was synonymous with the opposition to papal authority. And most of his native Germany was behind him.

Luther's excommunication was triggered by three books that he had published in 1520. These 'Reformation Treatises' calling for the reform of the church were considered heretical: in

Pierre Terrail, Seigneur de Bayard
(left) This epitome of French chivalry was dubbed 'the chevalier without fear and beyond reproach'. A resourceful commander, he led sieges under several monarchs, notably Charles VIII, Louis XII and Francis I. Captured by the enemy, he was twice released without ransom, so great was the universal respect felt for him. In 1521, Bayard held the fortress of Mézières – with only 1000 men – to enable King Francis I to expel the Imperial troops from French soil.

Suleiman the Magnificent
(right) Less than a year after ascending the Ottoman throne, the young Suleiman took Belgrade in 1521. Under his rule, the Empire reached the zenith of its glory.

Luther's German Bible
(above) In 1521, after his abduction by the Elector of Saxony, Luther was installed in the castle of Wartburg. There he stayed until March 1522. It was an intensely active period, taken up with a series of pamphlets and correspondence with friends and supporters. It also saw the translation of the Greek New Testament into vernacular German. The first edition was published in 1522.

The Diet of Worms
(right) From January to May, 1521, the Diet debated the bull of excommunication issued by Leo X and allowed Luther to appear before it to justify his actions. But he refused to withdraw anything he had written in his books, citing his conscience as his ultimate counsel. Although censorship followed, his beliefs spread rapidly throughout the Holy Roman Empire.

40

June 1520, Luther was given two months to recant or face excommunication. He did not recant.

Three weeks after the bull of excommunication was issued, the 21-year-old Catholic Charles V – King of Spain, and Holy Roman Emperor – opened his first 'Diet' (imperial council) at Worms in Germany. He summoned Luther to the Diet, giving him the chance to defend his doctrines or to withdraw what he had written. The Emperor offered Luther safe conduct to the city, and the monk made a triumphant entry. On April 18, Luther appeared before the Diet. He acknowledged that he had written the condemned books, but refused to withdraw a word: 'Unless I am proved wrong by Scriptures or by evident reason . . . I cannot retract and I will not retract. To go against the conscience is not safe, and is not right. God help me. Amen.' As

he left the hall, he raised his hand high above his head in a symbolic gesture of defiance.

The diet had not been the confrontation that Luther had hoped for. He had expected that King Charles would have collected 50 doctors of divinity to refute him in argument. But all they said was: 'Are these books yours?' 'Yes.' 'Will you recant?' 'No.' 'Then get out!'

KIDNAP

Since the Emperor had given Luther safe conduct to the Diet, he was allowed to leave freely. But the following months he was outlawed from the Empire. Luther's patron, the Elector Frederick of Saxony, came to his aid at this point: he had him

Jean-Loup Charmet

Mauro Pucciarelli

Archiv für Kunst und Geschichte

A fearless explorer
(above) This coloured map by Battista Agnese bears witness to the exploits of Ferdinand Magellan, captain of the first ship to circumnavigate the world. On April 27, Magellan was killed in a skirmish with islanders in the heart of the Philippines.

St Ignatius Loyola
(left) This was a watershed year in the life of Ignatius Loyola, 'the soldier of God'. Born in 1491, the youngest son of a wealthy noble family, he was a proud soldier. But in 1521 he was hit by a cannonball at the seige of Pamplona. Thereafter his life changed. His book, The Spiritual Exercises, *which he began while convalescing from his injury, became a religious classic, and the order he founded,* The Society of Jesus – or Jesuits – *a powerful weapon in the Counter Reformation.*

Mary Evans Picture Library

'kidnapped' on his way home to Wittenberg and hid him in the Saxon Castle of Wartburg until the spring of 1522. Here Luther let his hair grow and lived disguised as a minor nobleman 'Knight George'; he continued to write his religious tracts, and began his translation of the New Testament into German.

Luther's condemnation at Worms strengthened rather than weakened the spread of his beliefs. The secular rulers of Germany drew great advantage from the religious revolt. They looked on the efforts of Charles V to restrain Luther as an infringement of their own freedom, and insisted that they, not the Emperor, had the right to choose the religion of their states. They saw a chance to put an end to the power of the Church in their territories and to stop the flow of gold to Rome.

In several parts of Saxony, monks and nuns abandoned their monasteries, while in Wittenberg the townspeople overthrew altars and smashed images in churches.

LUTHER'S FOLLOWING

Even as far away as England, Luther was gathering a small following in the academic worlds of Oxford and Cambridge. But King Henry VIII refuted Luther, and Pope Leo X rewarded him for his loyalty with the title of 'Defender of the Faith'.

1521 also saw the start of the war between Germany and France. Competition between the two countries for England's support was high, but Charles V had the advantage. His aunt, Catherine of Aragon, was married to Henry VIII. On 25 August, Henry and Charles formed their alliance against France. England had the winter to prepare for war.

The ambitions of King Christian II
(above) Having acceded to the Dano-Norwegian throne, Christian began negotiations with the Swedes to form a Northern Union. But becoming impatient, he decided to fight for possession and had himself crowned in Sweden on November 4, 1520. Intrigue and the notorious 'Stockholm bloodbath' – in which over 80 Swedish bishops, nobles and burghers were killed – saw the infant union crumbling within the month. In January 1521 the War of Liberation began, which ended with the coronation of Gustavus Vasa as king of an independent Sweden in 1523.

Cortez gains control of the Aztec Empire
(left) Hernan Cortez's victory at Tenochtitlan on August 13, 1521, marked the fall of the Aztec Empire. The capital Montezuma was rebuilt and renamed Mexico city.

Archiv für Kunst und Geschichte

Archiv für Kunst und Geschichte

ÆTATIS SVÆ · LXXVII ·
· 1 5 5 0 ·

Scala

Self-portrait: Cranach in 1500/Uffizi, Florence

LUCAS CRANACH

1472-1553

From obscure beginnings Lucas Cranach became a celebrated and wealthy painter, second only to Dürer in the German Renaissance. For almost 50 years he served the Electors of Saxony at their court at Wittenberg, and owed much of his success to their enlightened patronage. He controlled a large studio which produced a huge output of beautifully finished pictures, many painted by his two sons.

Always in contact with scholars, Cranach played a leading part in bringing the ideas and artistic language of the Italian Renaissance to Germany, and from around 1515 was also the official painter for the Protestant cause. Yet his work never simply expressed Reformation or Renaissance ideas. His style was his own – provincial because of his geographic isolation and personal because of his unique vision of the world.

A Busy and Successful Life

Cranach rose from provincial obscurity to become court painter to the Electors of Saxony. But his association with leading figures of the Reformation did not prevent him enjoying wealth and prestige.

Key Dates

1472 born in Kronach, Upper Franconia

c.1501 arrives in Vienna

1505 enters the service of Frederick the Wise and goes to Wittenberg with him

1508 is granted a personal coat of arms by the Elector and visits the Netherlands to paint portrait of the future Charles V

c.1511-13 marries Barbara Brengbier

1525 sets up a printing firm

1537 elected burgomaster. Son Hans dies in Italy

1540 wife dies

1550 goes to Augsburg

1552 goes to Weimar

1553 dies in Weimar

Lucas Cranach took his name from the town of Kronach, where he was born in 1472. Kronach was an unimportant town in Upper Franconia, a part of the Holy Roman Empire ruled by the Church through the Diocese of Bamburg. Although only 15 miles east of Coburg, ruled by the Elector of Saxony, it fell into the cultural orbit of Nuremberg, an Imperial city some 50 miles to the south.

Almost nothing is known of Lucas' childhood or early training. His father was himself a painter, referred to in documents as Hans Maler, meaning 'Hans the Painter' and Lucas also took this surname in his early years.

TRAINED BY HIS FATHER

Hans was obviously successful, for he lived in a substantial house in Kronach's market square. None of his output has been identified, but we can presume that he worked in woodcut as well as producing devotional works for local churches and houses, and perhaps also carried out mural decorations. Lucas would have assisted and taken his training from him.

Lucas probably remained in his father's workshop, off and on, until around 1498, when he was 26. An unsubstantiated account suggests he went on pilgrimage to the Holy Land in 1493 in the entourage of Elector Frederick of Saxony and Duke Christopher of Bavaria. In this case, he would have visited Venice and Rhodes *en route*, but there is no

The artist's birth town
(above) Cranach took his name from the town of his birth, Kronach, and he stayed there until his mid-twenties, receiving his early artistic training from his father.

16th-century Vienna
(right) This German engraving shows the Imperial city as it must have looked when Cranach arrived there around the year 1501. It was here that he established his reputation as a painter, and developed his mature style.

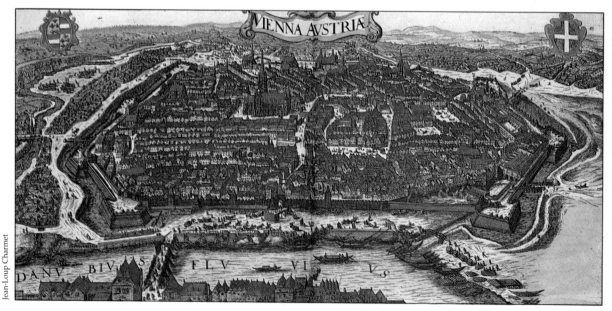

44

Vienna University
(right) Cranach mixed with the scholars associated with Vienna University, and even painted portraits of some of them. They helped introduce him to the new classical and humanist learning.

Archiv Gerstenberg

evidence in his later work of his having seen foreign landscapes. More certain is that he was in Vienna from around 1501. On the way there he would have passed through Nuremberg, where he may have encountered the work of Albrecht Dürer, one year his senior.

Although he was by now 30 years of age, no works by Cranach before this time have been identified. The first signed and dated works in Vienna show a mature talent, and by 1503 he was producing woodcut designs for the city's leading printer. These show a clear influence from Dürer's work in this medium, although Cranach invested them with a nervous intensity all his own. Vienna was far more advanced intellectually than Franconia, and Cranach soon joined the circle of

humanist scholars gathered around the university who were fired by Renaissance ideas emanating from Italy. Among his finest early works are portraits of Johannes Cuspinian, rector of the university, and his wife (this page).

IN THE SERVICE OF THE ELECTOR

In about 1504, Cranach's growing reputation as a painter and his association with progressive intellectuals from the university led to him being taken into the service of Frederick the Wise, Elector of Saxony. The Elector probably came across Cranach through the court in Vienna, where we can assume he was already carrying out work for the Emperor. In 1505, Cranach returned with Frederick to Wittenberg. This town on the river Elbe had been developed during the 15th century as the capital of Saxony, a region consisting largely of poor land, with scattered communities surrounded by expanses of heath and forest.

As part of the development and modernization of his domains, made wealthy by mining activities, Frederick the Wise founded a university at Wittenberg in 1502 and began the process of attracting influential scholars. In a sense, Cranach was one of these, his appointment intended to contribute to enhancing the prestige of the Elector as a rich and cultured ruler, inhabiting a magnificent palace decorated with fine works of art. This patronage gave Cranach status and stability and for almost 50 years he lived and worked in Wittenberg, producing hundreds of pictures and assuming an ever grander lifestyle. At some stage he married Barbara Brengbier, who came from Gotha and was five years his junior. They had five children, including two sons who

Dr Johannes Cuspinian and his wife Anna
(right) Johannes Cuspinian, an historian and rector of the University, was one of the scholars with whom Cranach associated when he arrived in Vienna. These two panels by Cranach bearing portraits of Cuspinian and his wife were probably painted to mark their wedding which took place in Vienna around 1502. The pictures are full of learned astrological symbolism. In the portrait of Johannes, the owl with a bird in its claws signifies that the sitter has a melancholic temperament. The falcon, heron and parrot in his wife's picture point to her sanguine character.

Colorphoto Hans Hinz

Colorphoto Hans Hinz

Oskar Reinhart Collection, Winterthur

Oskar Reinhart Collection, Winterthur

The Electors of Saxony

Cranach worked enthusiastically for three great Electors of Saxony through a period of intellectual and political ferment. Frederick the Wise came into the title in 1486, and transformed Saxony into one of the leading states in Germany. A religious man with scholarly interests, he founded the University of Wittenberg in 1502 and patronized scholars such as Luther and Melanchthon. Under Frederick's protection, the Protestant Reformation gained a foothold. His brother John the Steadfast succeeded him in 1525, and continued his policies with equal vigour. But John's son John Frederick the Magnanimous, Elector from 1532, had to face the backlash from Emperor Charles V. He was forced to submit to Imperial authority in 1547, but by this time the Reformation was too firmly established to be destroyed.

Ralph Klein Hempel

Kunsthalle, Hamburg

worked for many years in their father's workshop.

The first picture known to have been painted by Cranach in Wittenberg is the *Martyrdom of St Catherine* (p.51), which repeats a subject already painted during the Vienna period. As well as major commissions of this type, Cranach began the series of portraits of the Elector, his family and courtiers that would continue throughout the artist's entire career. In addition, he had responsibility for the decoration of the Elector's new buildings. He appears to have been an adaptable and diligent craftsman, ably controlling his assistants and thus capable of producing a large output of well-finished pictures. Other duties included the design of court dress and emblems for the armour of the royal guard.

From the limited evidence, we can see that Cranach enjoyed huge success in Wittenberg. In 1508, Frederick granted him a coat of arms – a winged and crowned serpent with a ring in its mouth. In the same year, he was sent by the Elector to the Netherlands where he painted the portrait of the 8-year-old Charles, future Holy Roman Emperor – a great honour. According to a story, while in the Netherlands, Cranach drew the likeness of Emperor Maximilian on a wall, remembered from Vienna, much to the amazement of those present who had seen the Emperor in the flesh.

From about 1508, Cranach painted an

Archiv für Kunst und Geschichte

The Cathedral Church
(left) Cranach's engraving of 1509 shows Wittenberg Castle Church as it looked when Luther nailed his famous 95 Theses to the door. The 15th-century building was largely destroyed by fire in 1760, and was subsequently rebuilt. The wooden doors no longer exist, but the bronze ones cast to replace them in the 19th century bear the text of the Theses. The interior contains the tombs of Luther and Melanchthon.

46

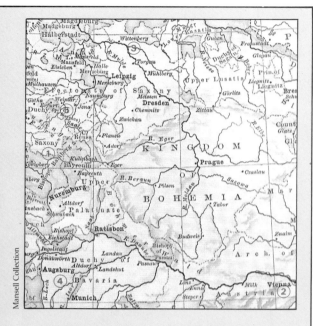

Cranach's patrons

(left) Cranach spent almost fifty years serving the Electors of Saxony. Here he uses the triptych form normally reserved for religious subjects to enshrine the memories of all three Electors in a single composition set against a background of Saxony's landscape.

The artist's travels

(above) Born in a small town in Franconia **1**, Cranach moved to Vienna **2** before embarking on his career with the Electors at Wittenberg **3**. He went to join John Frederick at Augsburg **4** in 1550, and followed him to Weimar **5** in 1552.

Luther sits for Cranach

(above) Cranach followed the Elector's lead in supporting the cause of the Reformation. He came to enjoy a special relationship with its leader, Martin Luther, and painted his portrait several times.

increasing number of subjects based on classical mythology, showing the importance of humanist ideas at the court. However, more far-reaching developments – ones that were irrevocably to change the whole Christian world – began to take place at Wittenberg. In 1508 Martin Luther arrived at the university to lecture on ethics. His radical ideas aroused great enthusiasm in Wittenberg and controversy throughout Germany. In 1517 he fixed his famous *95 Theses* to the door of Wittenberg Castle Church, vigorously attacking the corruption of the Church, and four years later the Pope excommunicated him. Throughout these turbulent events Luther enjoyed the protection of Elector Frederick the Wise, who at this dangerous juncture took him into hiding at Wartburg Castle where he began his translation of the Bible into German from Greek and Hebrew texts. Meanwhile Luther's supporters in Wittenberg, now led by Philip Melanchthon, began to put his ideas into practice.

CHAMPION OF THE REFORMATION

Cranach was undoubtedly involved in these events. He became friends with Luther and painted his portrait many times. He also produced the reformer's likeness in engraved and woodblock form for wide dissemination as part of the growing flood of Protestant propaganda. In supporting Luther, Cranach was entirely in step with the Wittenberg court, with the Elector of Saxony leading a movement of German princes to assert their independence from the Roman Church and to a lesser extent the Empire.

Cranach's friendship with Luther is difficult to assess, but a few letters survive in which Luther wished Cranach's family well in intimate terms, suggesting they were quite close. But Luther's teaching did not radically alter the direction of the

Modern Wittenberg

(right) The tall towers of the Cathedral Church dominate this view of Wittenberg. Cranach spent most of his life there, amassing wealth and enjoying much prestige. In fact, he was elected mayor in 1537, and held the post again in 1540 and 1543. All the important monuments of the Reformation in the town are still standing, including the Elector's Palace, Melanchthon's house and Luther's house.

The Town of Augsburg
(above) Cranach went to Augsburg in 1550 to join the Elector John Frederick during his captivity following the Battle of Mühlberg.

painter's work. If anything, the number of sacred altarpieces was increased, although with a greater concentration on scenes from the life of Christ rather than the legends of the saints. Luther's religion was not iconoclastic or egalitarian; his pious form of Christianity saw no objection to religious imagery and he advocated vigorous punishment for the rebels in the Peasant's War of 1524-25. He remained faithful to the Elector, like Cranach. Curiously to modern eyes – and this demonstrates the complexity of the conflict – Cranach felt free to continue to produce work for Catholic patrons, including Cardinal Albrecht of Brandenburg, who also patronized Grünewald.

Against this background Cranach went from strength to strength. As early as 1512 he owned several properties and in 1520 he set up a pharmacy with the Elector's personal physician Martin Polich as partner. He continued to acquire property, some of it away from the fashionable market square where he lived in a large house, and received considerable sums in rent. Indeed, he was obviously a successful businessman, perhaps making more money in other ways than he did as a painter.

A BUSY WORKSHOP

Cranach was now the master of a thriving workshop producing portraits, religious subjects and mythological scenes (which were often coyly erotic) for many important patrons in addition to the Elector and destined for churches and palaces

Cranach's Sons

Cranach's huge output required a large studio with numerous assistants, and his own sons were among his helpers. The eldest son, Hans, was apparently as good a painter as his father, but died in 1537 too young to assert an independent manner. The second son, Lucas the Younger (1515-86), probably ran the day to day affairs of the workshop from about 1540, and may have been responsible for the change in the Cranach signature at about this date. He was an inferior artist, with a tendency towards fussiness, and a less clear sense of pictorial design than his father. However, he kept tight control over the Cranach studio until well into his 70s, maintaining a high standard of work as a result.

all over Germany. There is evidence that he had a wine-selling business and he certainly cashed in on the boom that the Protestant Reformation brought to Wittenburg publishing.

In 1525, John Frederick I became Elector, and granted Cranach, the court painter, the right to set up a printing firm with Christian Döring, the court jeweller. Enthusiasm for the Protestant writings of Luther and others ensured success and very quickly Wittenberg took over from Leipzig as the leading publishing centre in the area. Cranach and Döring financed the publishing of the first part of Luther's Bible, an enormous undertaking, and in 1525 the partners succeeded in driving a rival printer out of Wittenberg. By 1533, the firm was less successful and Cranach, now sole owner, sold it. In 1528, according to tax returns, Cranach was one of Wittenberg's wealthiest inhabitants, with a property of a declared value of 4000 gilders. An indication of the splendour of his lifestyle is that when in 1523 the exiled king of Denmark, Christian II, came to stay at Wittenberg, he was housed in one of Cranach's properties.

The workshop, which must have employed numerous assistants including Cranach's sons,

Cranach's tombstone
(right) The spot where Cranach is buried outside the Jakobs Church in Weimar is marked by this memorial showing an effigy of the artist and his coat of arms.

was efficently run and had a vast output. In 1533, it accepted a commission for no fewer than 60 pairs of portraits of the two previous Electors. In 1537, Cranach was elected burgomaster or mayor of Wittenberg, a post he held again in 1540 and 1543. In 1537 he sent his eldest son Hans on a study tour of Italy. The young man was evidently a gifted painter whose work cannot really be distinguished from that of his father, but unfortunately he died while in Bologna.

JOURNEYS TO NUREMBERG

Cranach seems to have travelled occasionally in the 1530s himself, visiting Nuremberg for the third Imperial Diet and again in 1539 to escape a plague that was gripping Wittenberg. Documents tell that Cranach's wife died in 1540, but we do not know the circumstances. Cranach was now 68, but from the evidence of his pictures clearly still in full command of his powers. His younger son Lucas probably ran the studio on a day to day basis, but the father took responsibility for the most important commissions.

In the 1540s the struggle between the Catholic Emperor and the Protestant elector intensified and in 1544 Wittenberg was besieged. Remarkably, Cranach was summoned from the town on a safe conduct to see the Emperor, who wished to know who painted a Cranach picture in his possession – the father or one of his sons. In 1547, John Frederick was defeated in the battle of Mühlberg and was taken in captivity to Augsburg, where he was joined by Cranach. Peace was made and, in 1552, Cranach went with John Frederick, now a prince of the empire, to Weimar. There he stayed in the house of one of his daughters, still working off and on, until his death on 16 October 1553.

The Cranach signature
(above) This late signature is based on Cranach's coat of arms.

Stadtkirche, Weimar

Hans Cranach
(far left and left) The most gifted of Cranach's sons, Hans, died tragically young. This presumed self-portrait, and the delightful sketch of a monkey, show him to have inherited his father's powers of observation.

Lucas Cranach
(above) Cranach's influence on his sons was paramount. In this Crucifixion, Lucas bases the figures of Luther and Cranach the Elder on the far right on earlier portraits painted by his father.

'Swiftest of Painters'

As the most prolific and versatile artist of 16th-century Germany it is impossible to classify Lucas Cranach except by the title his talent, speed and efficiency earned him – 'the swiftest of painters'.

A great artist of the Renaissance in Germany, Lucas Cranach was at the forefront of the new, forward-looking intellectual currents that were undermining the traditions of medieval Europe. Yet he spent most of his career in an isolated northern town and was only indirectly affected by the perfect expression of those ideas practised in Italy. As a result, his works can look quaint and provincial when compared with those of his southern contemporaries, Giorgione or Raphael. But, in his own context, he was just as progressive as they, and in some ways a more individual artist, precisely because of his isolation.

Nothing is known of Cranach's early work in his home town of Kronach, and we have to wait until he was in Vienna and 30 years old to see anything certainly by his hand. The wonderful *Crucifixion* and the woodcut of *St Stephen* (both this

page), produced in 1502, show that he had learned a great deal from Dürer, while his portraits of scholars from the university, including the rector, Johannes Cuspinian (p.45), show he was already in intellectual circles and absorbing ideas from Italy.

Cranach's work at the time gained its power through a marvellous understanding of landscape, achieved through close observation of nature and through the expressive power of his figures. These may not be classically proportioned or posed, but they do show an extraordinary range of dramatic gesture and action, all learned originally from Dürer's woodcuts but developed with a nervous energy all Cranach's own.

Once in the service of Frederick the Wise in Wittenberg after 1505, Cranach's independent direction became even more marked. He adapted

Joachim Blauel/Artothek

The Crucifixion (1500)
(below) Although belonging to the 'Vienna group' this early Cranach painting may well have been executed before the artist's arrival in the city.

Archiv für Kunst und Geschichte

Cranach's woodcut designs
Dürer's influence can be seen in the woodcut designs Cranach made for Vienna's leading printers, such as this St Stephen *used in the* Missale Pataviense *of 1503.*

Kunsthistorisches Museum, Vienna

The Torgau Altarpiece (1509)
*(above) The balanced composition of this
painting, also known as* The Altarpiece
of the Holy Kinship, *may well have
been derived from Italian Renaissance
works which Cranach undoubtedly saw
on his visit to the Netherlands.*

Lucretia (1529)
*(right) The classical figure of Lucretia,
who stabbed herself to death after she was
raped, provided Cranach with the subject
of several of his works. Lucretia is
dressed, somewhat titillatingly, in the
fashion of the Wittenberg court.*

Städelsches Kunstinstitut, Frankfurt

Sarah Campbell Blaffer Foundation, Houston

Staatliche Kunstsammlung, Dresden

**Centre panel of The Martyrdom of
St Catherine (1506)**
*(above) Cranach's arrival at the court of
Wittenberg marked a radical change in*

*his style of painting. Unlike his earlier,
rougher brushwork, here, using a
pointed brush, he picks out fine features
such as brocade and jewellery.*

Archiv für Kunst und Geschichte

quickly to his role as court painter, falling in
easily with the sensibilities of his patrons. The
magnificent altarpiece of 1506 depicting *The
Martyrdom of St Catherine* (this page), for example,
combines realism and a sensual joy in the qualities
of colour, texture and line in a most complex and
animated scene.

Cranach's state visit to the Netherlands in 1508,
reinforced the influence of the Italian Renaissance
in his work. The so-called *Torgau Altarpiece* (this
page), for example, showing a grouping of the
Holy Family, has a more balanced composition, is
less cluttered and has figures with real weight and
solidity. Presumably the artists he met in the Low
Countries showed Cranach collections of
drawings and engravings from Italy. From this
time, too, we also see the first classical subjects in
his art. An engraving of 1508 has *The Judgement of
Paris* as its theme, with the nudity of the three
goddesses introducing what would later become
the artist's most characteristic subject.

Although excited by these developments, the
bulk of his work at this time was more
conventional. Frederick the Wise's court required
portraits, altarpieces and smaller devotional
paintings to decorate chapels, and these Cranach
began to produce in great number. The Elector and
court could not fail to approve of such works,
which were highly finished, sophisticated and
produced regularly and to order. His portraits, in
particular, showed members of the court in
wonderfully elaborate and fashionable dress.

Cranach was not a temperamental artist who
would keep frustrated patrons waiting years for a

Colorphoto Hans Hinz

Offentliche Kunstsammlungen, Basle

Virgin and Child with a Cake (1529)
(left) Set against the plain, dark background Cranach favoured in his later portraits, this exquisite work sums up the serenity and beauty of his Madonnas.

picture to be finished, but a highly professional manager of a workshop, proud of craftsmanship and efficiency. He clearly worked with a substantial team of assistants, yet there are no copies among the huge output. A painting might be done in different versions, but the master seems to have supervised closely and participated in almost everything, correcting details and carrying out the most difficult portions himself.

For portraits, Cranach would execute sketches in oil on paper from the noble sitters who increasingly demanded pictures from him and would then use these as a file copy from which repeated finished portraits could be produced over the years, varying the pose and costume without the necessity of another sitting. From 1520, this became even more necessary to meet the demand for portraits of Luther and the Saxon princes who led the Reformation.

SENSUOUS ENTERTAINMENT

From the later 1520s, the artistic mood we now call Mannerism began to spread from Italy. This

Joachim Blauel/Artothek

Discovering Eve

Dürer's great *Eve*, together with its pendant *Adam*, had an enormous impact on the artists of northern Europe. The engraved version of the painting was widely disseminated and through it artists caught sight of the new interest in the nude developing in Renaissance Italy. But northern artists could only partly respond to the monumentality and grandeur of Dürer's fully-fledged Classicist interpretation. Cranach, for example, took the subject to his heart, painting numerous exquisite nudes, but they are essentially decorative – pretty, contemporary and titillating women. Cranach thus founded another, alternative tradition to the Classical, one followed through in the late 19th century by Gustav Klimt whose sinuous line and glowing surface decoration echo Cranch for an even more overtly erotic effect.

Gustav Klimt
(1862-1918)
Adam and Eve
(1917-18)
(near right) Klimt's Eve dates from an era of fascination with the femme fatale *– triumphant in her powerful sexuality*

Albrecht Dürer
(1471-1528)
Eve (1507)
(far right) By contrast, Dürer's Eve with her coy, concealing fig leaf, conveys a sense of modesty and shame at her role in the Fall.

Galerie F. Welz

Österreichische Galerie, Vienna

Josef S. Martin/Artothek

Prado, Madrid

TRADEMARKS
Adornments

Lucy Su

Even when painting nudes, Cranach rarely passed up an opportunity to include fashionable extras such as the wide-brimmed hats or the heavy, gold chain necklaces worn by the wealthy.

Alte Pinakothek, Munich

The Golden Age (1530)
(above and detail right) One of two works of the same theme, this painting shows a number of naked men and women cavorting in naive merriment in a paradise-like walled garden. The detail of the lions shows Cranach's sympathetic treatment of animals, either tame in a garden – as here – or as the prize of the hunt.

signified a relaxation in the strictness of Renaissance classicism and a new concentration on the sensuous and the entertaining aspect of pictures. Cranach seems to have responded easily to this general trend for it more closely reflected his own artistic temperament. His portraits, particularly of women, became more idealized, with slender figures and small rounded heads. Their dress, in particular hats, became ever more obvious and in the latest fashion.

Gradually the sensuous nude, usually representing Eve, Lucretia or Venus, assumed a prominent place in Cranach's output. But these are no longer the classic nudes of the Renaissance: they are idealized court beauties titillatingly hiding their nakedness with transparent veils, or wearing jewellery or hats to accentuate their erotic availability. Meanwhile, his workshop continued the production line of portraits, devotional panels (now concentrating on themes acceptable to Reformation theology), mythological scenes and altarpieces. One of Cranach's last great works, painted in 1550 at the age of 77, was a self-portrait (p.43) stern and as realistic as anything he had painted. If there is anything to be read from his unnerving direct gaze, it is pride in a job well done.

THE MAKING OF A MASTERPIECE

The Judgement of Paris

Cranach returned to this poignant subject again and again, painting this exquisite, tiny version in 1530. He first tackled it in 1508 in an engraving that has essentially the same composition as the later paintings. Mercury comes down to earth and appears to Paris with three naked goddesses, from whom Paris must choose the fairest. Juno promises him wealth, Minerva offers victory in battle, but Paris chooses Venus, who offers him the love of any woman he selects. Deciding on Helen, Paris starts the Trojan war. Cranach misses none of the subject's erotic possibility – his Paris is a knight in armour, not the shepherd boy of the story, and the three goddesses vie with each other to show off their sexual attractions.

Staatliche Kunsthalle, Karlsruhe

Humorous horse
(right) Cranach's sympathetic rendering of animals can be seen here in his portrayal of Paris' prancing horse with its comical sidelong glance.

Metropolitan Museum of Art, New York

Mercury or old man?
(left) As a messenger to the gods, it was Mercury who was charged with leading the three goddesses to Paris to be judged. Traditionally Mercury was youthful, graceful and athletic. But in Cranach's works he appears as an old man, as if he were the Knight Paris' valet. In some versions, he is wearing peacock feathers which suggests that he is connected to the goddess Juno.

Original sketch
(right) This pen-and-ink sketch of the same theme is related to, although different from, the other painted versions.

Anton Herzog Ulrich Museum, Braunschweig

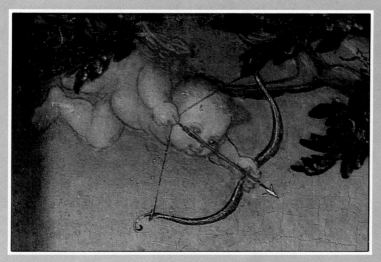

Cupid's bow
(above) Hovering in the top left corner of the painting is this chubby Cupid, ready to shoot his arrow when his mother, Venus, comes before Paris to be judged for beauty alongside the goddesses Juno and Minerva.

The choice is made
(below) In this later version, dated 1537, the story is a little further ahead. The choice seems to have been made, and Venus, presumably, has her hand on the prize – traditionally a golden apple but shown here as a decorated golden orb. Juno's association with peacocks could explain the strange attire of the bearded man.

Castle in the air
(above) A castle – imaginary or a patron's home – tucked away in the background, was a detail often included in Cranach's work.

New look Paris
(left) In mythology, Paris is portrayed as a shepherd, but here Cranach gives this popular subject a chivalric touch by attiring him in armour.

The three goddesses
(below) In the faces of these three goddesses, Cranach manages to convey the most alluring and subtle blend of innocence and coquetry.

Saint Louis Museum, Missouri

Gallery

The Penance of St Jerome
1502
22" × 16¼"
Kunsthistorisches
Museum, Vienna

The great scholar St Jerome (342-420) spent four years as a hermit in the desert, where he said he had 'only the scorpions and wild beasts for company'. Like many other ascetic saints (notably St Anthony), he had vivid sexual hallucinations, and he described how he would beat his chest until he had overcome them. He does not mention that he used a stone to chastise himself, but it became a convention to portray him holding one.

was virtually a picture factory at the height of his very successful career, he was such a skilled manager and craftsman that his standards remained high.

He tackled most subjects – from conventional religious subjects such as The Virgin of the Grapes to courtly commissions such as The Stag Hunt, and from mythologies such as The Judgement of Paris to humorous moralizing scenes such as The Fee. Although he excelled in so many fields, it is perhaps as a painter of alluring women that he is most memorable. Judging from the number of copies and versions, the Reclining Water Nymph and Judith were two subjects his contemporaries demanded continually.

The Rest on the Flight into Egypt *1504*
28″ × 20¾″ Staatliche Museum, West Berlin

The subject of The Rest on the Flight into Egypt gave artists the opportunity to portray the Holy Family in a landscape setting. Cranach was particularly interested in landscape early in his career, and here created an almost fairytale atmosphere with the lush foliage and brilliant, luminous colours. This is Cranach's earliest signed work – his monogram is on a stone in the foreground.

The Virgin of the Grapes *c.1525*
28½″ × 16½″ Alte Pinakothek, Munich

The grape was a common symbol in medieval and Renaissance painting. It symbolized the wine of the Eucharist and therefore the blood of Christ. St Augustine wrote 'Jesus is the grape of the Promised Land, the bunch that has been put under the wine-press', by which he meant that Christ's blood would be spilt.

Judith with the Head of Holofernes *c.1530*
33¾″ × 23¼″ Kunsthistoriches Museum, Vienna

Judith was a Jewish biblical heroine who infiltrated the camp of
Holofernes, an Assyrian general who was besieging her city. She
charmed him, got him drunk and then beheaded him. The story was
seen as symbolizing the triumph of virtue over vice, but also often
served as a pretext, as here, to paint a beautifully seductive woman.

The Stag Hunt *1529*
46½″ × 69¾″ Kunsthistoriches Museum, Vienna

Hunting was a favourite pursuit of noblemen and Cranach painted several pictures of the subject for his courtly patrons. This one shows the Emperor Maximilian I and the Electors Frederick the Wise and John the Steadfast among the hunters. Neither Maximilian nor Frederick were alive at the time the picture was painted, so it was probably commissioned by John the Steadfast. The high viewpoint has allowed Cranach to set out the various incidents of the hunt with almost comic-strip clarity.

The Garden of Eden *1530*
31½″ × 46″ Kunsthistorisches Museum, Vienna

In the foreground, God confronts Adam and Eve after they have eaten the forbidden fruit, and in the background Cranach has shown various other scenes from the Genesis narrative. From right to left, they are: the Creation of Adam, the Temptation, the Creation of Eve, the Discovery of the Sinners and the Expulsion from Paradise. Cranach was a brilliant painter of animals and seems to have enjoyed himself portraying the beasts in the Garden of Eden here, particularly the delightful bears.

The Judgement of Paris *1530*
13¾" × 9½" Staatliche Kunsthalle, Karlsruhe

In Greek mythology, the shepherd Paris was the judge of a celestial beauty contest, having to choose among the goddesses Juno, Minerva and Venus. He gave first prize to Venus, who bribed him by offering him the love of Helen of Troy. Cranach has represented the scene in contemporary costume and the three contestants are delicious coquettes rather than classical divinities.

The Fee *1532*
42½″ × 46¾″ National Museum, Stockholm

The theme of the ill-matched couple was a popular one in northern European painting of the Renaissance, building on the comic tradition exemplified most memorably in Chaucer's Merchant's Tale, where an old man, January, marries a young woman, May. The exact nature of the transaction taking place here is not made explicit, but the old man's expression makes it clear that it is not business he has in mind.

FONTIS NYMPHA SACRI SOM
NVM NE RVMPE QVIESCO ·

Lucas Cranach

Reclining Water Nymph
1537
19″ × 28½″
National Museum,
Washington

This was one of Cranach's most popular designs, for no fewer than ten versions of it are known. The theme of the reclining nude was developed in Venice at the beginning of the century, and Cranach may well have been influenced by engravings from Italy. The inscription reads Fontis nympha sacri somnum ne rumpe quiesco *(I, the nymph of the sacred spring, am resting here; do not disturb my sleep).*

Luther and the Reformation

Led by Martin Luther, the religious revolution known as the Reformation shook the supremacy of the Catholic Church in Europe and founded the beginnings of the Protestant faith.

Art was very closely connected with the beginnings of Protestantism. More than ever before, pictures were used to spread the new religious ideas, and close friendships developed between the artists and the reformers. Such was the case with Lucas Cranach the Elder and Martin Luther, an association which lives on today in Cranach's memorable portraits of the founder of the Protestant faith.

Martin Luther was born in November 1483, in the town of Eisleben in present-day East Germany.

He received a good education, and in 1501 went to study at the University of Erfurt where he gained a master's degree. In 1505, at his father's wish, he began studying law, but during the summer he was caught in a violent thunderstorm on the road near Erfurt and, prostrated by a flash of lightning and in fear for his life, vowed to become a monk.

Within two weeks Luther honoured his promise and entered the Augustinian monastery at Erfurt. For the next ten years or so he devoted himself to his theological studies and to his

The 95 Theses
(right) When Luther nailed his 95 Theses to the door of Wittenberg Castle Church on 31 October 1517, he was only following the customary way in which scholars in the university town invited learned debate. They were not the first set of propositions Luther had advertised in this way, nor did he think they necessarily contained revolutionary doctrines. But the attack on the sale of indulgences by the church was seen as an unforgivable assault on the Catholic hierarchy, and it started a chain of events that led to the eventual foundation of the Protestant Church.

An early home
(left) As a youth, Luther was sent to study at the St George school in Eisenach, which he later described as his favourite town. While he was there he boarded with the Cotta family, and their house has now been turned into a museum dedicated to his memory.

Zefa

Interfoto

All pictures this page by Archiv für Kunst und Geschichte

Lucas Cranach

Faithful followers
(above) Disciples helped Luther spread his doctrines throughout Germany. Melanchthon set down a systematic theology of Lutheranism, while Justus Jonas and Johannes Bugenhagen organized the new Church. Erasmus withdrew his support from Luther when he realized the revolutionary implications of his message.

Lutheran propaganda
(below) This woodcut of 1545 contrasts the true religion as preached by Luther on the left, with the teachings of the Catholic church, whose friars on the right are collecting money from the sale of indulgences.

promising academic career. In 1511, he was sent by his order to the monastery at Wittenberg, and became professor of theology at the university there the following year. It was in his lectures and sermons over the next six years that the ideas which formed the basis of the religious Reformation evolved.

A PERSONAL RELIGIOUS VISION

In these early years, Luther's search for deeper spiritual understanding was guided by his own personal temperament – he was highly strung, emotional and subject to bouts of depression – and by the religious beliefs of the time. He feared Hell, the Devil and the closeness of Judgement Day. Tormented by the belief that God's justice was punitive, he looked to the Bible for reassurance, and gradually developed his own interpretation of the righteousness of God – the doctrine of *Justification by Faith alone*. This doctrine was based on the belief that salvation is given to the individual believer by God through His grace, rather than as a reward for merit, which is inevitably tainted by sin, and therefore deserving of retributive justice. Since faith is personal, the

An appearance before Cajetan
In 1518, Luther was invited to Augsburg to appear before the Pope's representative. But the urbane Cardinal Cajetan could not persuade him to recant his heresy.

priest was no longer necessary as an intermediary with God – a premise which automatically challenged the entire Church system.

The notion of *Justification by Faith alone* was the core of Luther's theology and, as such, gave birth to Protestantism. But the revolution did not happen overnight, and until 1517 Luther carried out his responsibilities in Wittenberg seemingly unaware of the potential of his ideas. All this changed on 31 October 1517, when Luther translated his thoughts into action and nailed his *95 Theses* to the door of the Castle Church in Wittenberg, thus unleashing the religious revolution now known as the Reformation.

CHURCH CORRUPTION

Luther was furious about the sale of indulgences in Wittenberg. These were documents, sold by the Church, which offered remission of penance for a cash payment. The people flocked to hear indulgence sellers like John Tetzel, who attracted his audiences with the jingle: 'As soon as the coin in the coffer rings, the soul from purgatory springs!' Sentiments like these contradicted Luther's beliefs about salvation, and he deeply resented the Church taking money from the poor under what he understood to be false pretences. He criticized the system in the *95 Theses*, but could not have foreseen the consequences of his action. What he had intended as an academic debate rapidly became a national issue, and Luther was thrust from obscurity into the limelight.

Luther's protest immediately appealed to the Germans and aroused intense interest throughout the Holy Roman Empire and beyond. For years resentment at the greed of the Church had been growing, and now at last the people felt they had found someone to champion their cause. Luther's ideas were translated into German and printed pamphlets were sent all over the country. His skills as an author and preacher enabled him to convince thousands. The movement could not be ignored.

The Church attempted to silence Luther, but reacted too slowly. Theologians first attacked Luther's doctrines in the autumn of 1518. Thereafter the Church continually called for Luther to recant, but he refused to do so, believing in the truth of his doctrines. It became increasingly obvious that Luther's challenge was not a harmless call for reform. His doctrine opposed the entire theological basis of the Catholic Church and he found himself on a collision course with its authorities.

By 1520, the Church leaders realized that they had to take action, and in October Luther was sent a bull of excommunication. Fortified by the support of thousands, from princes to peasants, Luther ignored the Pope's message and defiantly set light to a bonfire made from the papal bull and theological books. The break with the Church was now irreparable. In January 1521, Luther was finally excommunicated.

THE DIET OF WORMS

A broadly based movement such as the Reformation could not distance itself entirely from politics. Luther was now banned by the Church, but his relationship with the secular authorities also had to be regularized. To be effective, the papal ban had to be reinforced by an imperial edict. Thus it was that the new emperor, Charles V, found Church reform to be the most urgent issue facing him at the Imperial Diet of Worms in the spring of 1521. Charles invited Luther to defend himself at the Diet and, on 16 April 1521, the Reformer arrived in triumph at Worms, to streets filled with thousands of cheering supporters. The following evening he appeared for the first time before the Diet and was asked to recant.

The next day, in a packed hall, Luther again faced the Emperor. Again he was questioned about his books, and had prepared a reply. He spoke first in German, then in Latin, using no notes. Luther acknowledged the writings as his own and justified them on the basis of truth, as they were grounded in the Word of God. He finished with the plea: 'Here I stand. I cannot do otherwise. God help me. Amen.' The Emperor replied: 'A single friar who goes counter to all

Burning the papal bull
(below and above) The sale of indulgences sanctioned by Pope Leo X launched Luther on his reforming crusade. When the Pope issued a bull of excommunication in 1520, Luther responded defiantly by publicly burning it in Wittenberg, along with books on canon law.

In defiance of the Emperor
(above) In 1521 Luther was summoned to the Diet of Worms to appear before Charles V, but the Emperor could not get him to change his ideas. The Diet denounced Lutheran heresy and placed Luther under imperial ban, making him an outlaw of both church and state.

Lucas Cranach

The Luther Altarpiece
(left) Luther is commemorated in Wittenberg by Cranach's altarpiece in the town church. The predella shows Luther preaching in front of the Crucifixion.

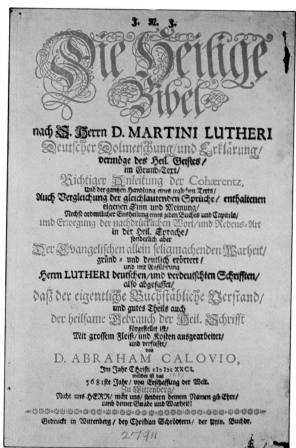

Christianity for a thousand years must be wrong.'

Luther continued in his defiance, and although the Diet issued an edict against him, the authorities were powerless to act. Luther's ideas had generated such excitement that to punish Luther would risk revolt. Some even feared for Luther's safety, and immediately after the Diet he was 'kidnapped' by his own followers and 'imprisoned' in the Wartburg Castle until the situation was calmer. All future attempts by the Catholic Church to deal with the Lutheran threat proved futile. Luther had triumphed at Worms, and the Protestant religion had come into being.

The remaining years of Luther's life were ones of consolidation for Protestantism. There were high points – such as the formulation of the Confession of the Lutheran faith at Augsburg in 1530 – and low points, particularly the crisis caused by the Peasant War of 1525, when extremists in the evangelical party incited the peasants to rebel against their masters. Luther's advice to settle grievances peaceably was disregarded and the peasants were savagely suppressed.

Luther himself found personal happiness in 1525, when he broke his monastic vows and married a former nun called Katherine von Bora.

He became a happy family man, content to write copiously and to preach, but was concerned also to steer his new creed through its early years. This religious genius, whose ideas had seized the popular imagination, died in February 1546, in Eisleben. Rarely has the course of history been altered so effectively by the actions of one man as it was by those of Martin Luther.

Cranach/Staatsgalerie Regensburg

A first Bible
(above) While he was hiding in Wartburg Castle following the Diet of Worms, Luther set himself the task of translating the Bible into German. Published in 1534, the text gave the Germans a good vernacular edition of the scriptures.

Luther's protector
(left) Frederick the Wise, Elector of Saxony, was responsible for Luther's appointment as professor of philosophy at Wittenberg University, and always had a protective attitude towards him. He refused to implement the papal bull against Luther, and arranged for his 'kidnapping' to Wartburg.

A Year in the Life 1547

In 1547 The Emperor Charles V won his great victory at Mühlberg over the Schmalkaldic League of Protestant Princes with serious consequences for the Elector of Saxony and his court painter Lucas Cranach. But the Protestant cause in Germany and in Scotland during this year was only in temporary eclipse.

Henry VIII of England and Francis I of France were two of the three great princes who dominated the European political scene during the first half of the 16th century. Both died in the early months of 1547. The third prince, the Emperor Charles V was to survive for another war-torn decade complicated by the political repercussions of the Reformation.

Charles V was absolute ruler of a huge empire 'on which the sun never set'. His dominions ranged from Aztec Mexico in the West, conquered for him by Hernando Cortés (who also died during 1547) to Austria in the East under his brother Ferdinand. This vast dominion, which even extended down into the Italian peninsula, had seriously alarmed the French King who had taken the unprecedented and, to some eyes, the even heretical step of allying himself with the Turks in the East. Although

Honoré Daumier/Sancho Panza and Don Quixote/Glasgow City Art Gallery and Museum, Scotland

Bridgeman Art Library

Marc Riboud/The John Hillelson Agency

Tilting at windmills
(above) Miguel de Cervantes, the Spanish playwright, poet and novelist, was born in 1547. He is most famous for his Don Quixote, the would-be knight who sets out with his loyal servant Sancho Panza in search of chivalric glory over a century too late.

Kabul recaptured
(right) The Great Moghul Humayun succeeded in wresting Kabul from his brother Kamran at this time.

Victory at Mühlberg
(above) The tenacious Holy Roman Emperor, Charles V, was determined to reassert his sovereign control over the dissident Protestant princes of Germany, many of which had banded together as the Schmalkaldic League under Frederick of Saxony, Cranach's patron. The league was defeated at Mühlberg in April 1547, and the rather obese Elector of Saxony was forced to surrender to the Emperor – to the ruin of his Saxon kingdom.

Pope Paul III had of necessity made an alliance with the Emperor, their relationship by 1547 was less than amicable.

Two years earlier the Pope had convened the Council of Trent which, dominated by the newly founded Society of Jesus, was to become the spearhead of the Counter Reformation. Meeting at Trent in northern Italy (modern Trentino) on Imperial soil, Protestant and Catholic representatives were invited from all over Christendom. The Pope was attempting to establish peaceful relations within Europe so as to present a united front against the Turks.

While Paul III saw the council as of doctrinal importance, Charles on the other hand had hoped it would be an excellent forum for sorting out the unification of Protestant and Catholic Germany. He was obsessed with establishing imperial supremacy over his German princedoms. Inevitably there were clashes between papal and imperial policies with the result that the council was moved from Trent to Bologna on papal authority in March 1547 – to the fury of the Emperor. There could be no hope of settling German religious problems on papal territory with a papal Council. An impasse was reached until the election of a new pope.

PROTESTANT DEFEATS

Charles now concentrated on suppressing the Schmalkaldic League of Protestant Princedoms which threatened his supremacy. He declared war on the League and succeeded in shattering it at the Battle of Mühlberg in April 1547. The capture

Louvre, Paris

Council of Trent
(above) This famous church council, inaugurated by the Emperor Charles V, was moved to Bologna by Pope Paul III when the inevitable impasse between Pope and Emperor was reached in 1547.

British Library

Protestant reformer enslaved
(left) John Knox discovered his vocation as preacher and spokesman of the Scottish Reformation while beseiged in St Andrews Castle with other Protestants in 1547. The governor of the town succeeded in recapturing the fortress with French aid and was no doubt quite happy to see Knox and others carried off into slavery by the French galleys, to be released 19 months later after English intervention.

New French monarch
(right) Henry II, second son of Francis I, succeeded to the French throne on his father's death early in 1547. His 12-year reign was a successful one at home and abroad though he lacked the brilliance of his father.

Fotomas Index

Giraudon

Jean Clouet/Henry II (detail)/Louvre, Paris

of the Elector John Frederick and his being forced to sign the capitulation of Wittenberg, the very heartland of Protestantism, was a blow from which Saxony never recovered. Cranach left Wittenberg to join his master in confinement at Augsburg. Nevertheless, no doubt to the artist's satisfaction, the Emperor's success was to be very shortlived.

Religion also played a large part in English politics during this year. Henry VIII died in January, leaving the throne to his nine-year-old son Edward. His uncle Edward Seymour (brother of Jane Seymour, Henry's third wife) assumed the position of Lord Protector. He pursued Henry's policy of trying to bully the Scots into a Protestant union through alliance by marriage to the young Edward VI. James V of Scotland had died five years previously leaving a week-old daughter from his marriage to the French aristocrat Mary of Guise. This infant was none other than the ill-fated Mary Queen of Scots.

Terrified of the continuation of the 'auld alliance' between Scotland and France, the English resorted to what was described as the 'Rough Wooing' hoping to win the young Scottish Queen by force. An able general, the Lord Protector defeated the Scots at the battle of Pinkie in September but was too late to save the Scots Protestants who were holding out in St Andrews Castle. French guns battered the castle into submission and the occupants, including the reformer John Knox, were carried off into slavery in French galleys. The worst blow was the capture of the young Queen who was promptly married the following year to the dauphin of France. Once more the wily Scots were a thorn in the side of the English.

French visionary

(left) The French astrologer Nostradamus began to make his prophecies around 1547. They were first published seven years later in verses grouped into hundreds or centuries. Still popular today, their somewhat ambiguous nature leaves many of the predictions open to wide interpretation.

Chambre Ardente

(right) Henry II's hatred of heresy led to the foundation of the 'chambre ardente' or burning chamber in the first year of his reign. 'Evidence' of heresy was no doubt supplied by the excruciating and ingenious torture methods favoured by the Inquisition.

Jean-Loup Charmet

Bibliothèque Nationale

Edimages

Coronation procession

(right) The nine-year-old Edward VI was crowned King of England at Westminster Abbey on 19 February 1547 after the death of his father Henry VIII. Edward's policies were initially dictated by his uncle, Edward Seymour, the Lord Protector, and then by the Duke of Northumberland, leaving posterity with little conception of the potential of the boy king who was to die after a six-year reign.

Bridgeman Art Library

Society of Antiquaries, London

SVI IPSIVS EFFIGIATOR

Æ: XLV.

Giraudon

Self-portrait: Holbein in 1543/Uffizi, Florence

HH HANS HOLBEIN

1497/8-1543

The son of a successful German artist, Hans Holbein worked in Switzerland before the religious turmoil of the Reformation caused him to leave for England in search of work. His first stay in London was spent among the circle of the great scholar and statesman Sir Thomas More. After a period back in Switzerland with his wife and family, Holbein returned to England, where he remained based until his death from the plague.

Holbein's phenomenal skill – particularly at portrait painting – was exploited by Henry VIII's secretary, Thomas Cromwell, who drew him into the king's employ. Soon, Holbein became Henry VIII's chief image-maker. Though little is known about his character, Holbein seems to have been a cultivated but cold man, who could switch his allegiance from More to Cromwell, the architect of the Royal Supremacy.

A German at the English Court

Hans Holbein moved to London permanently from his native Germany in 1532. His work soon found favour at court and he was appointed King's Painter. Holbein died in 1543 of the plague.

Very little is known about the life of Hans Holbein the Younger. Only a few dated documents and Holbein's works themselves – including some enigmatic self-portraits – provide us with clues to the personality of the man who became King Henry VIII's favourite painter.

Holbein was born in 1497/8 in Augsburg in Southern Germany. His father, Hans Holbein the Elder, was a gifted painter and had already carved quite a reputation for himself. Together with his elder brother, Ambrosius, the young Holbein trained for a while in his father's studio, and in 1514 the two boys were sent to Basel in Switzerland to serve their apprenticeships with the painter Hans Herbster.

In Basel, Holbein also worked for the publisher, Froben, producing book illustrations and a set of marginal drawings for Desiderius Erasmus's book *Praise of Folly*. This very important commission put him in touch with Basel's humanist circle, of which the scholar Erasmus was the leading light.

THE HUMANISTS

The humanists placed paramount importance on the intellectual pursuits, potential and well-being of mankind. Whereas medieval Christianity had taught the insignificance of man's earthly existence, the humanists believed in the value of human endeavours. They found the basis for their ideas in the literature and philosophy of the ancient Greeks and Romans, where the virtues of liberality, eloquence and wisdom were especially prized. Holbein seems to have gradually formed close friendships with some of the northern humanists, particularly Erasmus. Early on in his career his own humanistic interests were reflected in the sophisticated classical details he introduced into his designs and decorative schemes.

In 1517, and again in 1519, Holbein travelled to Lucerne, Switzerland, where he decorated the house of the town's chief magistrate in a splendid illusionistic style. At some point, probably in 1518, Holbein made a short trip to Italy where the work of the Renaissance painters Andrea Mantegna and Leonardo da Vinci made a profound impression on him. Once back in Basel, he soon showed

Like father, like son
Hans Holbein the Elder was a successful artist working in Augsburg. He painted this Baptism of St Paul *(1503-04) for a local convent. On the far right are the artist and his two sons, Ambrosius and Hans.*

Artothek

Staatsgalerie, Augsburg

Early training
(left) Augsburg in southern Germany, where Hans Holbein the younger was born. From an early age, he and his elder brother Ambrosius worked together in their father's studio.

Italian influence
(above) Holbein visited northern Italy around 1518 and probably stayed at Mantua. After this trip, the influence of Italian artists such as Leonardo is evident in Holbein's painting.

Key Dates

c.1487 born in Augsburg, southern Germany

1519 marries Elsbeth Binsenstock

1526 first visit to England; introduction to Sir Thomas More

1528 returns to Basel

1532 goes back to London

1533 paints *The Ambassadors*

1534 Henry VIII becomes Supreme Head of the Church; Thomas More imprisoned; Holbein paints *Thomas Cromwell*

1537 appointed King's Painter

1543 dies of the plague in London

himself to be a painter of great talent. He was extremely prolific, too, turning out portraits, altarpieces and designs for stained glass, as well as a series of huge frescoes.

In 1519 Holbein joined the painters' guild and rapidly achieved the status of chamber master. At this time he married Elsbeth Binsenstock, the widow of a tanner, who already had one son. In time they had two sons of their own, who became goldsmiths, and two daughters. It is assumed that

he also had a mistress, a certain Magdalena Offenburg, whom he painted in the appropriate guise of Laïs – the mistress of the legendary Greek painter, Apelles. Magdalena probably also modelled – somewhat less appropriately – for the Virgin in *The Meyer Madonna* (p.90).

In an astonishingly short time Holbein had become the foremost artist of the northern humanist movement. Among his finest works of this period are the three portraits he painted of Erasmus and a series of anti-clerical woodcuts illustrating the *Dance of Death*. In 1524 he visited France and expanded his artistic horizons. But two years later the violent impact of the Reformation brought religious painting in Basel to an abrupt halt and he was forced to seek prestigious commissions elsewhere.

INTRODUCTION TO THOMAS MORE

Armed with a letter of introduction from Erasmus to none other than Sir Thomas More and Archbishop Warham, Holbein left for England 'to pick up some angels' (coins), as Erasmus put it. He was welcomed by More in London and it is believed that he stayed at his Chelsea house for the remainder of his visit. Henry VIII had not yet begun his great programme of art patronage and so Holbein did no work for the Crown at this time, but he probably met the king, who was then in the habit of rowing down the Thames in his barge and calling on his close friend More without warning. More was then approaching the height of his political influence: the king relied on him both for company and advice, and he was soon to be made Lord Chancellor.

Thus, at a single bound, Holbein vaulted into the centre of political and intellectual life in

Swiss master
(right) Hans Herbster ran a workshop in Basel, Switzerland. In 1514, the two Holbein sons were sent to him to serve their apprenticeships.

Hans Holbein/Hans Herbster/Offentliche Kunstsammlung, Basel

Holbein's Humanist Friends

Holbein came into contact at an early age with the humanists in Basel and met Erasmus, a scholar and prominent member of the group. His portraits of Erasmus were much admired and led to a useful letter of introduction to Sir Thomas More in England. Through More, Holbein probably met Henry VIII; he certainly met More's influential circle of friends, whom he painted during his first trip to England, when he stayed at More's house in Chelsea.

Erasmus himself had stayed with More, most notably in 1509, when he wrote his great satire *Praise of Folly*, in which he wittily attacked the corruptions of the Church. The book was dedicated to 'his friend Thomas More', and was illustrated by Holbein.

Bridgeman Art Library

Helpful admirer
(left) Erasmus, painted in 1523 by Holbein. Erasmus was a leading light of the humanist movement and became one of Holbein's greatest admirers.

Powerful friend
(below) This is a copy of Holbein's portrait of Thomas More's family. In 1526, Holbein used a letter of introduction from Erasmus to meet More who was then about to reach the peak of his political influence.

Louvre, Paris

Rowland Lockey/National Portrait Gallery, London

England. He exploited his opportunity to the hilt. His sitters, all drawn from More's circle, included the king's astronomer and the Archbishop, who had himself painted in the same pose as Erasmus. The finest portrait of this period, and perhaps of all Holbein's English output, was that of More himself, conveying the man's aura of power as well as the sensitivity of his intellect. Still more impressive perhaps would have been his group portrait of the More family, but it has since been destroyed by fire.

In 1528, Holbein returned to Basel; he had only been granted a two-year leave of absence and a longer stay would have cost him his citizenship. Also, the Council had work for him. He bought two adjoining houses overlooking the Rhine and settled down to paint frescoes for the Town Hall. During this period he painted a sympathetic and intimate portrait of his wife and two of their children (opposite).

A RETURN TO LONDON

Meanwhile, the situation in Basel was rapidly worsening. The Lutheran faction was at its most extreme: Erasmus was forced to flee and iconoclasts destroyed nearly all the city's religious paintings in a single day. Holbein obtained some minor commissions decorating a tower clock in the city and designing patterns for goldsmiths, jewellers and glassmakers; he even made some costume designs. But the atmosphere was highly unfavourable to art of all sorts, and Holbein – although he supported the principles of the Reformation – decided to return to London.

He arrived late in 1532 to discover that events were moving very fast there too. Archbishop Warham had died and Thomas More, having refused to endorse the king's marriage to Anne Boleyn, had petitioned to resign the chancellorship. He was now trying to live in

Archiv für Kunst und Geschicte

DIE ALTE VND ERSTE STAT BASEL

Holbein's home in Switzerland
(left) Holbein's wife and children remained in Basel while the artist sought work in England. He returned there in 1528, but only stayed for four years.

imprisoned in the Tower, where he languished for another year while the Crown's agents, directed by Cromwell, prepared their case against him.

Though Cromwell was forbidding in appearance and character, qualities which are not shirked in Holbein's portrait, he was the most important patron Holbein could have acquired. During the next five years he not only filled the royal coffers with monastic gold, but orchestrated the most lavish propaganda campaign in the arts ever undertaken for the benefit of the Crown. One of the first jobs he gave Holbein was to design a woodcut for the title page of the Coverdale Bible, the first complete edition of the Bible in English. This showed Henry VIII delivering the Word to the bishops.

In July 1535 Thomas More was executed and in the following year Anne Boleyn was the first of Henry VIII's wives to lose her head. Holbein was

inobtrusive privacy and Holbein was obliged to turn to another source of patronage. This he found among the German merchants at the Steelyard, which was the London trading office of the Hanseatic League. At this time he painted a magnificent full-length double portrait *The Ambassadors* (pp.94-5), and the virtuoso *George Gisze* (p.86), both designed to attract the attention of Tudor court.

The status of his patrons rose quickly. By 1534 he was painting the king's secretary, Thomas Cromwell. In this same year More refused to swear the Oath of Supremacy, declaring that 'no parliament could make a law that God should not be God'. The king, who was now Supreme Head of the Church of England, had him cruelly

Religious extremists
(left) This woodcut illustrates the violent destruction of holy images during the Reformation. It was mainly the lack of religious commissions which caused Holbein to search for work in England.

Family group
(right) Holbein's wife, Elsbeth Binsenstock, whom he had married in 1519, and two of their children, Philip and Katharine. He painted this work in 1528 on his return to Basel.

The Artist as Propagandist

When Holbein was taken under the wing of his new patron, Thomas Cromwell, a formidable new propaganda team was born. Cromwell had clear ideas about how the Tudor monarchy and the Reformation should be portrayed to the public, and Holbein had the talent and the eye for just such a visual presentation. We see the court of Henry VIII through the eyes of these two men and they had a profound influence on attitudes to the monarchy at the time and for many years to come, illustrating the contemporary notion that 'Into the common people, things sooner enter by the eyes than by the ears, remembering better that they see than that they hear'.

National Portrait Gallery, London

The face of power
(above) *Thomas Cromwell, first Earl of Essex, after a painting by Holbein. Cromwell quickly became one of the most powerful men in England, masterminding the dissolution of the monasteries and greatly increasing Henry VIII's wealth and power. But he was found guilty of treason and executed in 1540.*

Tudor dynasty
(right) *An example of Cromwell's belief in artistic propaganda is clearly seen in this copy of a commemorative group of Henry VIII and his new queen Jane Seymour, with the king's parents behind. The original was a wall painting for Whitehall Palace, but it was destroyed in a fire in 1698.*

Reproduced by gracious permission of Her Majesty the Queen

The Royal Collection

now on the royal payroll, and in 1537 he was appointed the King's Painter. For an annual income of about £30, he performed a great variety of commissions for his royal master – from the design of his state robes to that of his book bindings. But he was chiefly valued for being 'very excellent in making Physiognomies'. By this time, the King had banned all religious painting.

Though he was a genius as a painter, as a man Holbein seems to have been shrewd, ambitious, ruthless and quite unscrupulous. Admittedly, the turbulent and bloody politics of those days made compromise and sudden switches of loyalty a virtual necessity for anyone close to the throne, even artists. But for all that, it is difficult not to be surprised by someone who was able to sell his talent to Cromwell, the man partly responsible for the death of More, Holbein's one-time friend, patron, host and sponsor.

A rare insight into Holbein's character (or his reputed character) comes from an anecdote told by the Flemish artist and art historian Karel van Mander. The story goes that Holbein was painting a portrait of a lady for King Henry, when a nobleman appeared in the room unannounced. The artist was so angered by the interruption that he flung the offending intruder downstairs – then hurried to offer his apologies to the king.

PAINTING THE KING

In the year 1537, Holbein was given his most momentous task when he was asked to paint a commemorative group portrait of Henry VIII, his new Queen, Jane Seymour, and the king's parents Henry VII and Elizabeth of York, which was to adorn the wall of the Privy Chamber above the throne itself. In the event, Jane Seymour died before the fresco was completed, having given birth to Henry's long-awaited and only legitimate son. 1537 was a year of shattering triumph for the Tudor dynasty. Henry managed decisively

Fotomas

Portrait of the artist
(above) A probable self-portrait of Holbein, dated around 1543. Little is known of his character, but he was certainly politically astute.

The Tower of London
(right) Holbein worked in the shadow of the Tower for most of his mature life. His first host in England, Thomas More, was imprisoned there in 1534.

German patrons
(below) The Triumph of Riches – a copy of a work commissioned from Holbein by the Hanseatic League, a group of German merchants who were the first people to employ Holbein when he returned to London in 1532. The allegory was designed for the banqueting hall of the German Steelyard's Guildhall to illustrate the temporary nature of wealth and glory.

to crush the most serious rebellion of his reign, the so-called Pilgrimage of Grace, and showed the Pope to be powerless to challenge his position as Supreme Head, next to Christ, of the Church of England. The great fresco was therefore conceived as a celebration of victory, peace and dynastic unity. Holbein had the job of enshrining in paint the official Tudor view of the immediate past.

We can only guess at the visual effect of his fresco – though every contemporary reference testifies to its awesome power – for in 1698 the negligence of a chamber maid caused the palace of Whitehall to be burnt to the ground.

Having completed the Whitehall wall painting, Holbein was sent abroad with the delicate task of painting likenesses of Henry's possible future wives. He visited Brussels where he painted a portrait of the delightful Christina of Denmark, which 'singularly pleased the king' and put him in a fine humour. However, political negotiations broke down, and Henry never married her. For a similar reason Holbein also painted a bland but pretty portrait of Anne of Cleves, whom the King decided to marry (though he later described her as 'the Flanders Mare').

In September 1538 Holbein returned once more to Basel and his family. A banquet was held in his honour and the city offered him a pension and other privileges in the hope of tempting him to stay permanently. But he did not linger. Though he was never naturalized, London had become his home as well as the centre of his career.

In his last years, Holbein painted less for the king, but there is no evidence that he fell out of favour. Indeed, his last, unfinished work was a large painting of Henry VIII granting the charter to the Barber-Surgeons' company. He also continued to work for the Crown by travelling abroad on diplomatic missions about which little is known.

DEATH FROM THE PLAGUE

Holbein's life was cut short by the plague which raged through London in 1543. The will he made in that year reveals that he was a resident in the parish of St Andrew Undershaft in the City of London, and that he left two illegitimate 'chylder wich be at nurse'. But despite Holbein's illustrious career, his will contains no mention of any property: only small items such as clothing and a horse. In fact he left several debts. But the debt which English art owes to the foreigner from Germany is far greater: he influenced the direction of English art for centuries to come.

A Perfect Likeness

Holbein's ability to achieve almost photographic realism in his painting made his reputation as a portrait painter, and has given posterity an invaluable record of the members of the Tudor court.

Hart Film

Freiburg Cathedral/Breisgau

The Oberreid Altarpiece (1521-22)

(left) Holbein painted the central panels of this altarpiece during his early years as an independent painter in Basel. It was commissioned by Hans Oberreid, a leading citizen of the town, who had recently married. His coat of arms and that of his new wife's family appear at the bottom of the painting, along with individual portraits of the family members. The panel on the left shows the Adoration of the Shepherds, *set among classical ruins symbolizing the Old Testament religion which was replaced by the new era of Christianity. To the right is the* Adoration of the Magi *set in less grandiose ruins.*

Sir Henry Guildford (1527)

(right) Guildford commissioned this portrait to commemorate his election to the Order of the Garter. He wears the collar of St George and the Dragon to indicate his membership of the Order, and holds the staff that shows his official position as Comptroller of the Royal Household. Guildford was a favourite of the king: his pose is suitably self-confident, while the way in which his bulky figure fills the picture space gives the portrait an impressive sense of authority.

Reproduced by gracious permission of Her Majesty the Queen

The Royal Collection

Holbein's reputation is based on the brilliantly observed portraits which he painted in England during the reign of Henry VIII. Their realism is astonishing even today, and it is easy to understand the reaction of Holbein's friend, the great scholar Erasmus, when he received the artist's drawing of Sir Thomas More and his family: 'It is so completely successful, that I should scarcely be able to see you better if I were with you.'

Yet Holbein did not start his career as a portrait painter. He trained in his father's workshop in Augsburg and that of Hans Herbster in Basel, where he not only learnt the techniques of oil painting, but also those of book illustration and the decorative arts. Holbein's early paintings were mainly monumental and religious works, stylistically in the Northern tradition of Dürer and Grünewald. By the late 1520s, a new influence can be seen. In *The Meyer Madonna* (1526, p.90), the Northern emphasis on sharply observed realism and incisive line is evident, but the classical motifs, calm symmetry and use of *sfumato* to soften the Madonna's features show a debt to Italian Renaissance art – particularly that of the great master, Leonardo da Vinci.

Many of Holbein's early religious works were probably lost during the violent iconoclasm (destruction of holy images) of the Reformation. This movement also put paid to a major source of potential income – church commissions – which is why Holbein was forced to leave Basel in search of work in England.

MORE AND HIS CIRCLE

Holbein already had quite a reputation for portraiture in England, since his portrait of Erasmus had been presented to Archbishop Warham. And most of his first visit to England (1526-1528) was spent mainly in the production of portraits of More and his circle – most of whom knew Erasmus. These are among the most astonishing likenesses in the history of art, and would certainly have astounded their Tudor sitters – who had never seen anything like them before. *Sir Thomas More* (p.92) is perfect in both its draughtsmanship and its apparent solidity – in Holbein's art, line defines form. More's face has been scrutinized and reproduced with an almost photographic accuracy – even down to the silver-tinged stubble on his chin. And Holbein's vision is so penetrating that his realism is not only skin deep: the slightly tensed brow above the tranquil eyes reveals More's thoughtful character.

Holbein's painting depended upon his phenomenal drawing ability. And it seems that, for him, drawing could be an end in itself, not merely a preliminary to painting. At first, his drawings were executed in chalks, which were sometimes heightened with water-colour. But after his return to England in 1532, the delicacy of this technique was replaced by the more vigorous and emphatic medium of ink. The collection of

Metropolitan Museum of Art, New York

Miniature portraits
(below) Holbein was a skilled miniature painter as this portrait of Anne of Cleves *attests. But whereas contemporary miniaturists such as Lucas Hornebolte worked in the tradition of medieval manuscript illumination, Holbein's miniatures were scaled-down Renaissance portraits.*

Victoria and Albert Museum, London

Stadelsches Kunstinstitut, Frankfurt

Margaret Wyatt, Lady Lee (c.1540)
(above) This portrait shows the sister of the Tudor poet Sir Thomas Wyatt aged 34, as the Latin inscription behind her indicates. It is typical of Holbein's late works in its three-quarter view, half-length pose, flat background and Latin inscription.

Simon George (1534-5)
(left) This portrait is unusual for Holbein because the sitter is shown in profile – an appropriate view for the circular, medallic shape of the painting. It differs from the preparatory drawing (p.85) in two main ways: in the drawing George has just started to grow a beard, while in the painting, it is fully grown. And in the painting he holds a flower.

drawings at Windsor are among Holbein's most popular works.

Part of Holbein's assured mastery of line was his ability to capture a likeness very quickly. It is known, for example, that he was only granted a sitting of three hours for his portrait of the *Duchess of Milan* (p.98). This was enough for him to make a 'very perfect likeness'. During his first English visit, he was not inundated by commissions, and could presumably take longer, but once he entered royal service, such swiftness of execution would have been necessary to supply increased demand.

A MECHANICAL AID

It has been suggested that Holbein may have made use of some sort of mechanical aid to allow him to record the outline of the sitter's face as fast as possible. Again, this would presumably only have been necessary during his second visit to England. If he did use a mechanical aid, it may have been a kind of tracing apparatus, of the type other artists such as Dürer and Leonardo are known to have used. This consisted of a peep-hole and a pane of glass. The artist looked through the peep-hole and glass directly at the sitter – rather in the way that the sights of a rifle are used to ensure a perfect line of vision – and traced the outline of the sitters' features on to the glass with an oil crayon. The outlines would then be transferred on to paper.

The paintings themselves were executed on wooden panels, to which Holbein would transfer his drawings using a grey wash. He then worked up the painted surface with meticulous accuracy, often using notes on colour and jewellery details to help him attain a perfect reproducton of what he had originally observed.

In the first years of Holbein's second visit to England, when he was still hoping to attract royal favour, he often made a point of showing off his ability to record stunning likenesses – not only of faces, but also of surface textures. In his portrait of the German merchant *George Gisze* (p.86) the lush folds of pink velvet are set against the woven intricacies of the Turkish rug with an almost tangible realism. And as if to hammer home the point, Holbein has placed a bunch of carnations in a thin glass vase which is painted with exquisite accuracy, and through which are seen the stems of the flowers and the woven threads of the rug.

A CHANGE IN STYLE

George Gisze is also characteristic of this particular phase in Holbein's art in the abundance of props which surround the sitter as attributes of his profession. About three years after this particularly 'flashy' painting, Holbein's portraits altered in a most dramatic way. The compositions themselves became simpler, with the sitters placed against plain backgrounds of blue or green. The lack of depth in these backdrops is often accentuated by Latin inscriptions, placed on either side of the sitter's head, usually indicating the date and his or

The Windsor Drawings

One of the jewels of the collection of the Royal Library, Windsor is a group of some 80 drawings by Holbein. These studies probably remained in the artist's possession till his death, and subsequently found their way into the Royal Collection. At this time, they were bound in one lavish volume: an inventory of 1590 mentions 'a great Booke of Pictures doone by Haunce Holbyn of certyne Lordes, Ladyes, gentlemen and gentlewomen of King Henry the 8 his tyme . . . which booke was King Edward the 6.' They are among the most popular of Holbein's works.

William Warham, Archbishop of Canterbury (1527)
(right) This drawing in coloured chalks dates from Holbein's first stay in England, and is one of his most penetrating character studies. Like all of his drawings, it was made for a practical purpose – as a preparatory sketch for a portrait which the Archbishop sent to his friend, Erasmus. The freedom of the handling and the delicate use of soft crumbling chalk on white paper, are typical of Holbein's early style.

Anne Cresacre (1526-8)
(left) Holbein's drawing of Thomas More's ward is one of several portrait studies made for his destroyed masterpiece The More Family Group. *A free variant on Holbein's original composition (p.78) shows Anne standing second from the left.*

John More the Younger (1526-8)
(right) Anne was betrothed to Thomas More's only son, John – the fourth figure from the left in the family group. This study clearly demonstrates Holbein's left-handed shading: the bold chalk strokes incline sharply from left to right.

Simon George of Quocoute

(below) *The drawings that date from Holbein's second English period (from 1532 onwards) reveal a marked change in style. Holbein has now taken to using a pale pink or carnation primed paper, and the soft outlines are often reinforced in ink, creating a bolder and flatter effect. This new, simplified style may be due to the tracing apparatus that the artist began to use as a quick and economical aid to capturing the likeness of a sitter as rapidly as possible.*

Thomas Boleyn (c.1535)

(above) *In this majestic 'painted' drawing, Holbein used a variety of media – coloured chalks, indian ink and water-colour washes. The incredibly fine detail of the face and the free handling of the drapery make this a most striking portrait.*

An Unknown Lady

(left) *Here, Holbein's original chalk drawing (possibly of the Princess Mary) has almost been obscured by later attempts at retouching and rubbing out.*

85

Staatliche Museen, Berlin

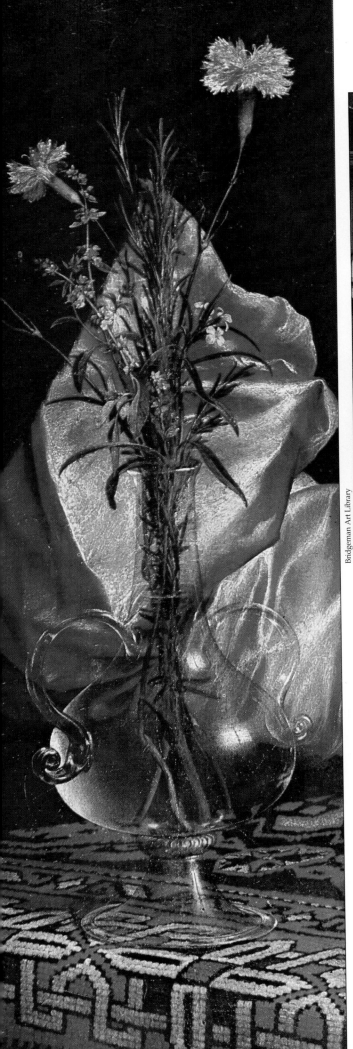

Bridgeman Art Library

George Gisze (1532)
(above and left) In this virtuoso portrait, Holbein depicts the German merchant surrounded by a dazzling array of objects, most of which are related to his occupation. The stunning vase of flowers may have had some specific relevance to Gisze, but it was probably included to show off Holbein's impressive technical skill.

her age. The plain backgrounds serve to heighten the impact of the portraits themselves.

The flatness of composition became particularly pronounced in many of the half-length portraits which Holbein executed of and for Henry VIII, where it was accompanied by an increased emphasis on linear patterning. In his portrait of *Henry VIII* (p.96), for example, the predominance of line is still evident, but it is put to a more decorative purpose. The sumptuous patterns of Henry's doublet and jewels, the flattened arms, and the head and hat almost cut out against the blue background all combine to create an icon-like image – appropriate for a monarch who was also the Supreme Head of the Church of England. Although the face is as individualized as that of Sir Thomas More painted nine years previously, the effect of the painting is entirely different. *Sir Thomas More* is a portrait of a man, *Henry VIII* is an image of god-like majesty.

It was Holbein's ability to create such spectacles of power that won him the chance to paint his most prestigious work, the Whitehall fresco. For the king did not want a family portrait, he wanted an image of absolute authority that combined physical might with symbolic legitimacy.

It is an irony that Holbein's consummate achievement has not existed for nearly 300 years – it was destroyed in a fire in 1698. But the surviving

TRADEMARKS

Objects and Inscriptions

The portraits which Holbein painted before his entry into royal service around 1535 are very different from those he executed during the last eight years of his life. In his earlier works, Holbein often surrounded his sitters with physical objects which indicated their official position or had some actual or symbolic relevance – as in *The Ambassadors* (see p.89). In the later works, the display of significant objects is replaced by plain backgrounds of blue or green. Often, these are adorned with Latin inscriptions written in gold capital letters indicating the year or the sitter's age: *aetatis suae 54* means 'aged 54'.

copies (see p.80) and cartoon (p.100) leave no doubt that the bloated, bulging, pig-eyed figure of Henry VIII must have been awe-inspiring. Visitors to the palace were said to be 'abashed' and 'annihilated', and many believed they were in the presence of the king himself.

In his cartoon for Henry's portrait, Holbein shows him turning slightly towards the queen, Jane Seymour; in the final painting, however, the king confronts the spectator directly. Obviously, Holbein's rendering of him was not designed to flatter, it was designed to glorify and magnify. The impression of raw power and indomitable energy is created partly by the sheer bulk of the figure, and partly by the contrast of Henry's challenging, virile pose with the more spiritual calm of the other three figures, whose eyes do not engage the spectator's.

ART AND PROPAGANDA

Holbein achieved these affects by using a whole range of artistic devices, but most of all he drew on the recognizable vocabulary of religious painting. The way in which the group is posed, for example, is reminiscent of the standard Renaissance arrangement for a Madonna and child flanked by saints. Holbein translated the language of religion into that of politics, and for the Holy Family he substituted the royal family. In this way he was able to create an image which simultaneously demonstrated the political supremacy of the Tudor dynasty, and the supremacy of Henry himself as head of the Church in England. In the process, Holbein had combined art and propaganda.

COMPARISONS

Images of Majesty

Monarchs often depended on their court artists to present their 'public image'. Holbein created what has become the archetypal image of Henry VIII, and the French artist François Clouet portrayed his king, Henry's contemporary Francis I, in a similar way. While the portrayals of Henry and Francis are aggressively male, Henry's daughter Elizabeth I ensured that portraits of her reinforced the image of a semi-divine virgin which she cultivated.

Nicholas Hilliard (c.1547-1619)
Elizabeth I (c.1600)
(left) Elizabeth I allowed her artists only to depict her as an ageless beauty. Bedecked with jewels, she appears like an object of worship.

François Clouet (c.1510-1572)
Francis I (c.1541)
Francis I established a reputation as a powerful but cultured king. The pose and composition of this portrait is very similar to Holbein's images of King Henry VIII.

Victoria and Albert Museum

Bridgeman Art Library

Louvre, Paris

The Ambassadors

Jean de Dintevelle (who appears on the left) commissioned this spectacular portrait (see pp.94-5) of himself and his friend, the bishop Georges de Selve in London in 1533. The first impression is of startling realism, but the painting has a surprising symbolic meaning.

The Ambassadors explores the relationship between art, time, achievement and death. In the painting, Holbein has 'frozen' time at a specific moment: the sundials indicate that it is 10.30 am on 11 April, while inscriptions indicate the sitters' ages. The young men are shown at the height of their powers: an array of objects symbolizes their accomplishments. But though art can stop time, in the real world death is inevitable. And between the men's feet is a distorted skull – a symbol of mortality.

National Gallery, London

'In the midst of life we are in death.'

Church of England Prayer Book

Dinteville's dagger
(above) Jean de Dinteville grasps a dagger in a gold sheath on which AET SUAE 29 is embossed, indicating that he is in his 29th year. De Selve's age – 25 – is written on the book on which he is leaning.

Layers of meaning
(right) The lute is a symbol of music, one of the seven liberal arts. But its broken string may be one of the many references to death in the painting.

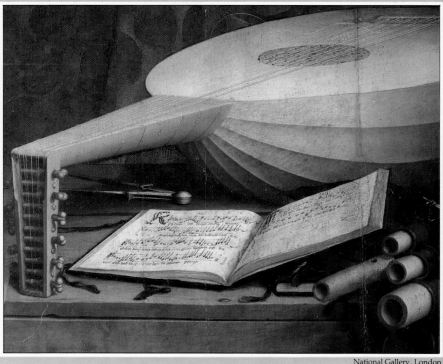

National Gallery, London

Symbols of Renaissance learning

(left) Holbein borrowed some of these instruments from his friend Nicolaus Kratzer, the king's astronomer. Astronomy, Geometry and Arithmetic were three of the seven liberal arts taught at university.

The pavement at Westminster

(below) The mosaic floor on which the two men stand is a loose copy of the 13th century pavement in the sanctuary at Westminster Abbey.

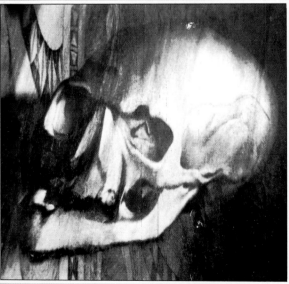

The hidden face of death

(above) This photograph shows a 'rectified' view of the distorted skull between the men's feet. It appears like this when the painting is viewed from the right – presumably it was approached from this angle when it hung in Dinteville's chateau. Cleverly distorted 'perspectives' were popular in Tudor times, but this particular image may have had special relevance for Dinteville: his personal 'device' was a skull, which appears on the badge on the hat he is wearing.

Symbolic Objects

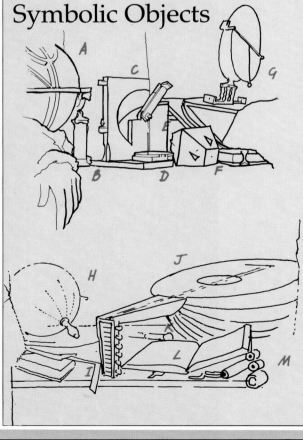

The objects in the painting are symbols of the sitters' wide range of knowledge. Music, Arithmetic, Geometry and Astronomy – the 'Quadrivium' taught at university – are all illustrated.

A celestial globe
B portable sundial
C table quadrant (for measuring altitude)
D astronomical instrument
E simple quadrant
F polyhedral sundial
G instrument for finding position of celestial bodies
H terrestrial globe
I arithmetic book
J lute
K pair of compasses
L hymnbook, with a Lutheran hymn, perhaps indicating Georges de Selve's sympathy towards Reformed religion
M case of flutes

Gallery

The clarity and precision of Holbein's art make him one of the most powerful portrait painters of all time. Even his early religious works such as The Meyer Madonna are characterized by minutely observed realism. This altarpiece is also typical of Holbein's painting in its cool colours and sharply defined outlines.

Artothek

The Meyer Madonna *1526-30*
57½″ × 40″
Schlossmuseum, Darmstadt

Jakob Meyer probably commissioned this altarpiece in the year his two sons (who appear with him to the left of the Madonna) died in childhood. Kneeling opposite are Meyer's daughter Anna, his wife Dorothea and his dead first wife Magdalen Baer (shown behind Dorothea). Holbein's mistress Magdalena Offenburg probably posed for the Virgin. The painting has both German and Italian features: the cool realism and linear precision are in the German tradition, while the symmetrical 'Madonna of Mercy' composition, the classical motifs and the softened features of the Madonna originate from Italian Renaissance painting.

Lady Guildford was one of the first portraits that Holbein painted during his first visit to England. His most brilliant achievement of this period is the sensitive portrait of Sir Thomas More. The charmingly informal Unknown Woman with a Squirrel was also painted during these years.

The masterpiece of Holbein's second English visit is the stunning double portrait known as The Ambassadors, painted before Holbein entered royal service. When he did, his style changed dramatically: Henry VIII and Queen Jane Seymour are hieratic images set against plain backgrounds. A similarly bold simplicity of design also distinguishes Christina of Denmark and Unknown Lady.

Mary Wotton, Lady Guildford
1527
31½″ × 25½″
St Louis Art Museum

This is a companion portrait to Sir Henry Guildford (p.82) – also painted in 1527. The date of the painting and the sitter's age (she is 27) appear as if cut in stone above the ornate pillar beside her. This placing of the figure beside classical architecture is typical of Holbein's early portraits. The artist has paid meticulous attention to detail, particularly in the dress, but has created a bold composition, with clear outlines, strong colour contrasts and an impressive sense of bulk. A preparatory drawing exists which shows Lady Guildford smiling, with a vivacious sideways glance.

Sir Thomas More *1527*
29″ × 23″ Frick Collection, New York

*This superb portrait of Holbein's friend, host and patron shows More
in his late 40s, wearing the 'SS' collar that was his badge of office as
Lord Chancellor. Breathtakingly accurate in detail, the composition
has a monumentality and simple grandeur appropriate to the sitter's
status and strength of character.*

Unknown Lady with a Squirrel *c.1526-28*
17¼″ × 15″ Houghton Hall, Kings Lynn

*This lady was probably painted during Holbein's first visit to England:
she is shown in the same half-length, three-quarter view as Sir Thomas
More, while the twisting foliage is similar to that behind Lady
Guildford. The painting's charm derives mainly from the bird, and the
little pet squirrel which sits on her arm.*

The Ambassadors *1533*
81½″ × 82½″ National Gallery, London

This magnificent , life-size double portrait shows Jean de Dinteville, a French aristocrat and ambassador to London and his friend and fellow-diplomat Georges de Selve, the young bishop of Lavour. The two men stand either side of a 'whatnot' on which lies an immaculately painted still-life display which symbolizes their intellectual and spiritual accomplishments. At first the painting appears to be a glorification of man's achievements, but it takes on another meaning when the distorted object which hangs between their feet is recognized as a skull. One of the several references to death in the painting, it makes the portrait a **momento mori** *(a reminder of death): its message is that despite man's worldly achievements, we all must die.*

King Henry VIII *1536-37*
10¾″ × 7½″ Thyssen-Bornemisza Collection, Lugano

*The only portrait from life of the king that is undoubtedly by Holbein,
this picture may have formed a pair with a portrait of Henry's
third queen, Jane Seymour. In this icon-like image, the body is
flattened up against the picture plane, and the emphasis is on
decoration: the gold thread, chain and buttons are painted in real gold.*

Queen Jane Seymour *1536-37*
25½″ × 15¾″ Kunsthistorisches Museum, Vienna

This timid-looking ex-lady-in-waiting had only become queen in the year that this portrait was begun. The next year, she fulfilled Henry's dream by bearing him a son (Edward VI), but died in childbirth. Like the king, she is set against a plain blue background, while her dress is painted in exquisite and precise detail.

Christina of Denmark, Duchess of Milan *1538*
70½″ × 32½″ National Gallery, London

A prospective bride for the king, following Jane Seymour's death, the widowed duchess sat for Holbein in Brussels on the afternoon of 12 March 1538, when the artist drew her likeness in a three-hour sitting. In this impressive full-length portrait, the young woman's fresh and delicate beauty is highlighted by her austere mourning clothes.

Unknown Lady *c.1540*
29″ × 20″ Museum of Art, Toledo, Ohio

This young woman used to be identified as Henry's fifth queen, Catherine Howard, but she was probably a member of the Cromwell family. Like the Duchess of Milan, she is placed against a plain greenish background, on which she throws a shadow. The gold inscription indicating her age echoes the gold details of her dress.

The Legend of Henry VIII

Henry VIII inherited from his father a country that was prosperous and stable after decades of civil war. He made his own image a crucial factor in strengthening still further the power of the monarchy.

During the reign of King Henry VIII (1509-47), Englishmen had their first significant contacts with the Renaissance, the new outlook in life and art that had first appeared in Italy and was gradually spreading throughout Europe. Henry himself welcomed Renaissance artists such as Holbein and the Italian sculptor Pietro Torrigiano, and patronised the 'New Learning' of scholar-writers such as the Dutchman Erasmus and England's own Sir Thomas More. In the early part of his reign Henry enjoyed playing the part of the ideal Renaissance monarch – handsome, cultivated, extravagant, warlike, and above all the absolute monarch of his realm. With age, corpulence and ulcers, much of the King's glamour disappeared, but his mastery in the state had become greater than ever. Henry, the man of many wives and many executions, was the first 'Tudor despot'.

Henry was the second of the Tudor monarchs. His father, Henry VII (1457-1509), founded the dynasty by defeating Richard III at the Battle of Bosworth in 1485. This brought to an end the thirty-year Wars of the Roses, during which aristocratic factions had made and unmade kings with alarming frequency. Henry VII was not a colourful figure like his son and other descendants, but he commanded respect and succeeded in restoring royal authority. Astute, persistent, hardworking and a first-rate businessman, he made his nobles keep the peace and greatly enriched the royal coffers.

Henry VIII was more erratic and lavish in his spending than his father, whose carefully

An image for posterity
(right) The archetypal image of Henry VIII was created in Holbein's dynastic portrait. The painting is destroyed, but part of the majestic cartoon survives. The formidable frontal pose was repeated in endless copies and variants.

Domestic pleasures
(left) This informal view shows the king playing the harp to his jester. Henry loved music, and tradition has it that he composed the famous song Greensleeves.

National Portrait Gallery, London

Hampton Court
(above) Cardinal Wolsey began this magnificent building in about 1515. Henry was angered at being outdone by one of his subjects, and Wolsey gave him the palace hoping to appease him.

Centre of a dynasty
(below) This window at Hampton Court shows Henry like a religious image. He is flanked by the coats of arms of his six wives and stands above those of three of his children.

The king's minister
(right) Cardinal Wolsey was the dominant figure in English government from 1515 to 1529. His failure to secure Henry's divorce sealed his downfall, and he died while under arrest.

accumulated fortune he soon frittered away. But he maintained the policy of strengthening the Crown, both practically and symbolically. Like his father, he employed 'new men' from outside the nobility – men whose loyalty could be relied on, since they owed everything to him. At the same time, Henry made the court a magnet for the nobility, encouraging them to compete for decorative offices and signs of the king's favour, so that they became psychologically dependent on him and spent less time on the estates which constituted their bases of power. Splendid ceremonies emphasized the special character of the king; and – a small but significant fact – Henry ceased to be addressed as 'Your Grace', like previous monarchs, and became the first to be called 'Your Majesty'.

MOCKING THE POPE

Hampton Court became Henry's favourite residence and he lavished money on it. His additions included the majestic Great Hall and a court for the game of 'real tennis' (that is, 'royal tennis'), a forerunner of the modern game. The palace was the scene of two of his weddings (to Catherine Howard and Catherine Parr) and his son Edward was born there in 1537.

The minister who organized all this for Henry was Thomas Cromwell, another 'new man', the son of a brewer and blacksmith. He developed the Tudor administration into something that resembled a permanent and specialized civil service. Wales was integrated into the English system in the mid-1530s, and later on Henry promoted himself from 'Lord' to King of Ireland.

Hampton Court, London

But the king – or his advisers – knew that the drastic religious changes he had introduced when he separated England from the Church of Rome were bound to confuse and alienate many people. To counteract this, they launched a large-scale propaganda campaign in the 1530s that was clearly intended to reach all classes. Plays and pageants explained the changes, mocked the pope and played on popular anti-clericalism; there was even a mock-battle on the Thames between papal and royal barges which ended with the 'pope' and his 'cardinals' getting a good ducking. Lawyers and moralists published pamphlets and books that exploited the rising tide of nationalism, making loyalty to England – and the king – the supreme value. And efforts were made to raise the status of kingship even further.

A PASSION FOR BUILDING

Now head of the Church, Henry was presented as, in effect, a semi-divine being. When Holbein, normally so perceptive and realistic, was called on to paint the King's portrait, he represented him as

The Dissolution of the Monasteries

(right and below) The monasteries were one of the great bulwarks of the papal system, so they represented a threat to Henry's authority after he had declared himself head of the English church. He appointed his chief minister Thomas Cromwell to carry out a programme of suppression and confiscation that left many monasteries to fall into ruin.

The Tudor triumph

(right) This allegorical painting shows Henry VIII on his deathbed handing over the succession to his son Edward VI. The pope lies crushed and beaten at young Edward's feet, symbolizing the Tudor triumph over Rome.

Robert Harding Associates/Ian Sumner

Fotomas Index

a cold and fearful icon rather than a man; or, as a contemporary put it, 'not only a king to be obeyed, but an idol to be worshipped'. In another of Holbein's works – a miniature – Henry appears as Solomon under an inscription reading 'Blessed be the Lord thy God, which delighted in thee to set thee on his throne, to be King for the Lord thy God.' And, for more popular consumption, Henry was shown on the engraved titlepage of Cranmer's Great Bible, enthroned like a divinity while he distributed 'the word of God' and multitudes below shouted 'Vivat Rex'! (Long live the King!).

The royal idol also advertised his greatness by building on a large and lavish scale. Wolsey's sumptous houses at Hampton Court and York Place (later Whitehall) were taken over and expanded into great royal palaces, and in Surrey a palace with a fairytale skyline, Nonsuch, was built from scratch to rival the famous French Renaissance château of Chambord. Nonsuch and York Place are now destroyed, but Henry's portions of Hampton Court remain among the glories of English architecture.

THE BREAK WITH ROME

During Holbein's first visit to England (1526-28), Henry was in his mid thirties but still had something of the playboy about him. Tall and powerfully built, he revelled in his athletic skills,

National Portrait Gallery

Catherine of Aragon

Henry VIII's first wife was the widow of his elder brother Prince Arthur. She was intelligent and capable and bore Henry six children, but all except Mary were stillborn or died in infancy. Henry's desire for a male heir made a divorce from Catherine imperative.

Unknown artist/National Portrait Gallery, London

and was also an accomplished musician. Effective power was exercised by Cardinal Wolsey, a 'new man' (reputedly the son of a butcher) who ran the government while the King jousted and hunted.

By the time Holbein returned in 1532, everything had changed. Wolsey was dead, and the king involved himself far more closely with policy. Wolsey was doomed mainly because he failed to obtain a divorce for the king. After many years of marriage to Catherine of Aragon, Henry had only a single child, the Princess Mary. This seemed to threaten the entire Tudor achievement, since everybody knew that no woman could govern properly, and that chaos, civil war or foreign occupation would inevitably result. (Of course Henry's younger daughter, later Elizabeth I, was to show that 'everybody' was quite wrong.)

Desperate for a male heir, Henry convinced himself that his marriage was invalid (for Catherine had been the wife of his dead brother), and put his case to Pope Clement VII. The situation was complicated by politics as well as theology (the Pope played for time, since he was a virtual prisoner of Catherine's nephew, the Emperor Charles V), and by Henry's love for Anne Boleyn, who insisted that he prove it by marrying her. Eventually Henry took matters into his own hands, breaking with the Pope, making himself Supreme Head of the English Church, and marrying Anne.

Ironically, then, the weakness in the Tudors' political system – the succession – brought about a series of events that tremendously enhanced the royal authority. In effect, Henry became pope as well as king; and the Royal Supremacy which excluded papal power from England also ended the independence of the English Church, whose courts at last became answerable to the civil power. Furthermore, the vast wealth of the medieval church restored the royal finances when Henry dissolved (that is, closed down and took over) the thousand or so English monasteries, confiscating their accumulated wealth and extensive lands.

A GODLIKE FIGURE

Henry's reign was far from an unqualified success. He had six wives, executed two of them, divorced two more, and had still not secured the succession beyond doubt. When invasion threatened, possible claimants to the throne were removed by judicial murder. Ill-judged wars bankrupted the Crown, and tampering with the currency seriously damaged the economy. Yet Henry's propaganda campaign worked. We still see the King through Holbein's eyes, as a splendid godlike figure; and the strengthened Tudor state bequeathed by Henry to his successors stood the test of revolutions and counter-revolutions over the three reigns that followed.

Cranmer's Bible

(below) As Archbishop of Canterbury, Thomas Cranmer declared Henry's first marriage invalid and crowned Anne Boleyn queen. The Bible issued under his auspices shows the king in almost divine splendour.

Bible Society, London

103

A Year in 1533
the Life

The year was dominated by the events surrounding King Henry VIII's quest for a male heir. Convinced that Catherine of Aragon was incapable of producing a son that would survive, Henry set about securing a divorce that would free him to marry Anne Boleyn. To do so, he had to split England from the Church of Rome.

By the beginning of 1533, Anne Boleyn was pregnant, a fact which precipitated a crisis in Henry VIII's matrimonial affairs. He had for some years been anxious to obtain a divorce from his first wife, Catherine of Aragon. His brother's widow, and six years older than Henry, Catherine had given birth to six children, but only Henry's daughter Mary had survived.

Henry desperately wanted to produce a male heir and convinced himself that the deaths of Catherine's children were God's punishment for an improper marriage. Under normal circumstances, Pope Clement VII would probably have obliged Henry's request for a divorce – the papacy was understanding in such cases and especially when they involved matters of state. But Catherine was the aunt of Charles V, Holy Roman Emperor, who, quite apart from feelings of family loyalty, had

Nicholas Hilliard: Queen Elizabeth I/Victoria and Albert Museum, London

Jean-Loup Charmet

Bibliothèque Nationale, Paris

Elizabeth I
(above) The future Queen Elizabeth I was born on Sunday 7 September 1533. She was not the son and heir whom Henry VIII so desperately wanted and for whom he divorced Catherine of Aragon, married Anne Boleyn, and split England from the Church of Rome. But Elizabeth was later to become one of England's greatest monarchs.

Gargantua visits Paris
(above) The French author François Rabelais wrote his daring satires on politics and religion – Gargantua *and* Pantagruel *– in the 1530s: the Sorbonne, the University of Paris, condemned* Pantagruel *in October 1533.*

Pope Clement VII
(left) In September 1533, the pope gave into pressure from the Emperor Charles V and threatened to excommunicate Henry VIII from the Church – four months after Henry's marriage to Anne Boleyn.

Edimages/Georges Goldner

very high moral standards and would not hear of a divorce. The sanctions which the emperor could bring to bear on the papacy far outweighed any pressure that the king could exert.

So the solution to his problem lay in the king's own hands. He had in any case fallen in love with Anne Boleyn and, knowing her to be pregnant, married her secretly on 25 January, thus ensuring that his son would be legitimate and the acknowledged heir to the throne.

THE QUESTION OF MARRIAGE

But the question of Henry's marriage to Catherine remained unresolved. There was no hope of obtaining a divorce from Rome, so it had to be achieved through the Archbishop of Canterbury. As luck would have it, the archbishop's chair was vacant: Archbishop Warham had died only the previous year. The king appointed Thomas Cranmer, a brilliant young Cambridge scholar of divinity who had, as one of the king's chaplains, been canvassing support for a divorce.

On 30 March, the new archbishop was formally consecrated. Although he took the usual oath of obedience to the pope, he qualified it by a formal assertion that he was not bound to do anything contrary to the law of God or to the king, realm, laws, and prerogatives of England. This, together with the hurriedly passed Act in Restraint of Appeals, which recognized the English primate as the ultimate authority for English ecclesiastical law without reference to Rome, cleared the way for Henry's divorce.

Mary Evans Picture Library

The death of Ariosto
(above) The poem Orlando Furioso *was written by the Italian author, Ludovico Ariosto, who died in 1533. The poem is regarded as the perfect example of Renaissance thought and classicism and had a great influence on European literature. This illustration shows a scene from* Furioso.

Redbeard the pirate
(below) Redbeard was a famous pirate who, in 1533, became admiral in chief of the Turkish Ottoman fleet. He made the North African coast a centre for piracy and united Algeria and Tunisia under Ottoman rule.

Mauro Pucciarelli

Topkapi Museum, Istanbul

Photo Goldner/Edimages

Inca civilization destroyed
(left) The Incas had settled in the Peruvian highlands around Cuzco from the 12th century and had developed one of the most advanced ancient Indian civilizations. But a civil war weakened their defences to the Spanish invasions, led by Francisco Pizarro and Diego de Almagro. Within just one year, (1532 to 1533) the Spaniards had taken complete control.

Immediately after his consecration, Cranmer presided over a meeting which decided that Henry's marriage to Catherine was contrary to divine law, and on 10 May he opened his court at Dunstable. Catherine refused to recognize Cranmer's authority to try a cause that was before the papal court and did not attend. On 23 May, the archbishop passed sentence, pronouncing that the pope had no power to license marriages such as Henry's, and that the king and Catherine had never been husband and wife.

Five days later, Cranmer declared Henry and Anne Boleyn lawfully married, and on 1 June Anne was crowned queen in Westminster Abbey. On 11 July, in a belated effort to protect the dignity of the Church, the pope prepared the sentence of excommunication which was delivered in September. Henry had, in effect, broken any remaining links with Rome: the Reformation in England was under way.

The king's personal desires in this matter were, coincidentally, in accordance with the aspirations of his people who, in a wave of nationalism and disillusionment with the Church, were keen to rid themselves of the influence of Rome. In other matters there was no such accordance. Catherine's humiliation was deeply resented by the people, Europe was shocked, and pope and emperor had been insulted.

But the final irony of this tale did not become apparent until three months after Anne's coronation. In the afternoon of Sunday 7 September, Queen Anne gave birth to a daughter. On the following Wednesday, the child was christened Elizabeth – the future Queen Elizabeth I of England.

Catherine de' Medici's marriage

(right) In 1533 Catherine married the Duke of Orleans, who in 1547 became Henry II of France. Catherine was a member of the powerful Medici family in Florence, and during the reign of her son, Charles IX, she managed to take over the government of France.

The new Archbishop of Canterbury

(below) Thomas Cranmer was proclaimed the first Archbishop of Canterbury of the new Church of England in March 1533. In May he declared Henry VIII free from his marriage to Catherine of Aragon and pronounced him legally married to Anne Boleyn.

Scala/Vasari/Wedding of Catherine de' Medici and Henry II/Palazzo Vecchio, Florence

Ivan the Terrible

(right) In 1533 Ivan was proclaimed grand duke of Muscovy at the age of three. He took over the government himself in 1544, aged only 14, and was crowned tsar in 1547. Under his rule, the state of Muscovy destroyed the Tartar domination of Russia and expanded east, beyond the Urals and into Siberia. He also made important trading contacts with the West. The later years of his reign were marked by periods of extreme ruthlessness and cruelty.

Jean-Loup Charmet

National Portrait Gallery, London

Bartholomeus Spranger: Portrait engraving of Bruegel

BRVEGEL

c. 1525-1569

The greatest Netherlandish artist of the 16th century and an accomplished draughtsman and engraver, Pieter Bruegel the Elder is mostly remembered for his lively peasant scenes. His detailed and sympathetic observations of everyday peasant life earned him the nickname 'Peasant Bruegel', but in fact he had influential patrons and cultured friends, and was probably an educated, sophisticated man.

Bruegel's paintings reflect the religious and moral preoccupations of the time. With his move from Antwerp to Brussels, his early crowded scenes gave way to the impressive landscapes and vigorous figures of his most memorable works, painted during the last five years of his life. These large-scale oils elevated landscape painting to a new eminence, and paved the way for the Dutch Masters of the 17th century.

The Flemish Enigma

Bruegel is popularly known as 'Peasant Bruegel' because of his marvellous portrayals of country life. But the little that is known of his life suggests he was a literate and cultivated man.

Bruegel's public image today is not unlike the one he enjoyed during his lifetime. Modern ephemera – Christmas cards, calendars, record sleeves – have made his paintings as familiar to today's public as the engravings of his works were to his contemporaries. Despite this, however, our knowledge of his life is disappointingly limited.

The few contemporary records that refer to him inform us that he was enrolled in the painters' guild in Antwerp in 1551, that in 1563 he moved to Brussels, where he married Mayken Coecke, the daughter of his former master, and that he died and was buried there in 1569. We have no clues as to his parents, the manner of his upbringing, or his early education. There are no letters, no diaries, and no first-hand written records of his beliefs.

AN OBSCURE LIFE

Even the date and the place of his birth are unknown, although informed guesses can be made as to both. As he was made a master in the painters' guild in 1551, it is highly probable (presuming he followed the normal course of apprenticeship) that he was born between 1525 and 1530. And as an Italian writer referred to him in 1567 as 'Pietro Brueghel di Breda', the town of Breda, then in the duchy of Brabant, is accepted by most scholars as the likeliest place of his birth.

The most important early source of information

The Low Countries
Bruegel's homeland was often politically unstable. Belgium did not become independent until 1831; before then it was ruled by various foreign powers.

Key Dates

c.1525 born, probably at Breda

c.1545 apprenticed to Pieter Coecke van Aelst in Antwerp

1551 becomes a master in the Antwerp painters' guild

1552-3 travels in Italy; probably works with the miniaturist Giulio Clovio in Rome

1555 designs engravings for the publisher Jerome Cock in Antwerp

1559 paints *Netherlandish Proverbs*

1562 visits Amsterdam

1563 marries Mayken, daughter of Pieter Coecke, and settles in Brussels

1564 birth of his first son, Pieter the Younger

1565 paints a series of pictures on *The Months*

1568 birth of his second son, Jan

1569 dies in Brussels

on Bruegel is the brief biography of him in *Het Schilderboek* (The Book of Painters), written by the Flemish painter Karel van Mander and published in 1604. This is a lively account, peppered with anecdotes, but in some ways it is more misleading than helpful, as it creates the image of Bruegel as essentially a comic painter rather than the profound and varied master he was. It is not surprising that Van Mander should foster the idea of Bruegel as the illiterate purveyor of a crude, rustic humour, as by the time he wrote, most of the master's paintings had been absorbed into private collections and his fame rested, to a large degree, on copies of his peasant scenes by his elder son and on the engravings executed early in his career.

Van Mander tells us that Bruegel started his career as a pupil of Pieter Coecke van Aelst (1502-

View of Naples (detail)

(below) This splendid panorama of the Bay of Naples is the only surviving painting connected with Bruegel's trip to Italy in the early 1550s. It may have been painted in Italy, although some authorities think it was done from drawings after Bruegel returned to the Netherlands. Most of the painting is topographically accurate – the massive, round-towered building is the Castel Nuovo – but Bruegel has altered the shape of the jetty from rectangular to circular.

Edimages

Detail; The Port of Naples/Doria Pamphili Gallery, Rome

Trading centre of Europe

(above) Bruegel spent most of his career in Antwerp, which at the time was one of the richest cities in the world. Its prosperity depended on its great port, which drew trade from all over Europe. Works of art played an important part in the export trade; in 1567, 300 artists were recorded in the city.

The artist's workshop

(below) In the busy workshops of Antwerp, painting was as much an industry as an art. Here, apprentices are grinding colours and copying a classical bust while the master paints a picture of St George and the Dragon.

his paintings. The translation of the famous architectural treatise of Sebastiano Serlio that he issued in 1545 was particularly important in spreading the ideals of Italian Renaissance architecture in northern Europe.

JOURNEY TO ITALY

Bruegel was only little affected by the Italian influence that characterized Coecke's paintings as well as his books, but soon after being enrolled in the guild of painters he set out on a tour of Italy. This was the normal thing for an ambitious young Flemish artist to do, for painters who could work in a style that showed acquaintance with the latest developments in Italy – 'Romanists' as they were called – tended to gain the best commissions.

Our knowledge of Bruegel's journey comes mainly from drawings and a painting he made during it. He seems to have spent some time in the studio of a miniaturist called Giulio Clovio in Rome, perhaps collaborating with him as a landscape specialist, and then proceeded further south to Naples, Reggio di Calabria and Sicily, before embarking on the leisurely return journey to Antwerp in 1553.

Ironically, the long-term benefits of Bruegel's

50), one of the leading artists in Antwerp. At this period, the city was enjoying a golden period of prosperity and expansion. As the approaches to Bruges silted up, it took over as the leading port in the Low Countries, inheriting the commerce of Venice and the Hanseatic League, and becoming an important stage in the Portuguese spice routes to the east. The population doubled in the first half of the 16th century and the growth of a flourishing export trade in art works drew artists from all parts of the country.

Antwerp's reputation as a printing centre also increased enormously. It produced over half the books issued in the Low Countries and began to rival the international status of Paris and Lyons. Bruegel's teacher Pieter Coecke was more distinguished for his publishing activities than for

BBC Hulton Picture Library

An Intellectual Friendship

The only known comment on Bruegel by an acquaintance is contained in the *Album Amicorum* (Album of Friends) of the geographer and cartographer Abraham Ortelius (1527-98). Writing four years after Bruegel's death, Ortelius described his friend as 'the most perfect painter of his century'. Bruegel's acceptance in the circle of a man of such high standing gives the lie to the idea that he was just a country yokel. Ortelius' tribute tells us that Bruegel 'was snatched away from us in the flower of his age. Whether I should attribute this to Death who may have thought him older than he was on account of his supreme skill in art, or rather to Nature who feared that his genius for dexterous imitation would bring her into contempt, I cannot say.'

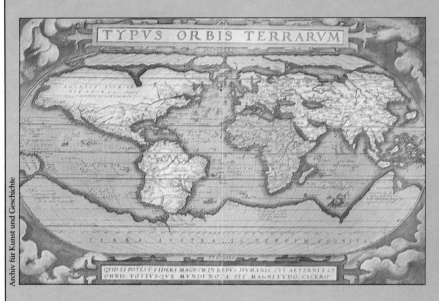

Archiv für Kunst und Geschichte

A portable world
(above) This world map is typical of the clarity and beauty of Ortelius' publications. His most famous work was Theatrum Orbis Terrarum *(Theatre of the Orb of the Earth), first published in 1570, which contained 70 maps. A friend wrote that Ortelius had 'made the world portable'.*

A great cartographer
(right) Ortelius trained as an engraver and turned to map-making under the influence of his friend Gerardus Mercator, the famous geographer. He wrote several learned geographical books and was a widely respected figure.

Bildarchiv Preussischer Kulturbesitz

D.G. Farquhar/Fotobank/England Scene

trip were to come not from Italy itself, but from the spectacular experience of crossing the Alps. Their grandeur fired his imagination and Van Mander, in an often cited passage, described the result: 'it was said of him, when he travelled through the Alps, that he swallowed all the mountains and rocks and spat them out again, after his return, on his canvases and panels, so closely was he able to follow nature here and in her other works.'

DISCIPLE OF BOSCH

This quality was to be fully exploited by Jerome Cock, an engraver, printer and editor who employed Bruegel from 1555, publishing a series of 12 large landscapes based on the young painter's designs. Cock's printselling business, 'Aux Quatre Vents' (At the Sign of the Four Winds), was an international concern by this time. His own taste was for the fashionable Italianate style and it has been suggested that he had prompted Bruegel to travel south, with a view to adding him to his stable of Romanist artists.

In the event, Bruegel's talents were channeled in another direction. The late 1550s saw a revival of interest in the symbolic fantasies of Hieronymus Bosch. The latter had died in 1516, but pastiches of his work continued to sell readily long after his

H. Roger Viollet

Homage to Bosch
(right) This engraving after a Bruegel drawing was published in 1557 with an inscription saying the 'inventor' was Hieronymus Bosch. This was an attempt by Bruegel's publisher to cash in on the popularity of Bosch's weird fantasies.

An Alpine journey
(left and right) Bruegel's journey to Italy had a profound influence on his art, but it was his passage over the Alps rather than the experience of Italy itself that left its mark. He made several drawings of the spectacular scenery and on his return to Antwerp he designed a series of 12 magnificent landscape engravings reflecting his experiences.

death, and Bruegel's employer seems to have set him to tap this lucrative market. Certainly, Cock's eye for profit is confirmed by the inscription 'Hieronymus Bos Inventor' engraved at the foot of Bruegel's *Big Fish Eat Little Fish* – a flagrant attempt on the publisher's part to pass off the print as an original by Bosch. Bosch's influence is visible also in some of Bruegel's pictures. However, Bruegel's commitment to this style was strongly linked to his service with Cock, and after his move to Brussels in 1563 his interest in both the subject matter and the format of such works waned appreciably.

Bruegel's career in Antwerp must also have been affected by his friendship with Abraham Ortelius, although here the influence is much harder to pin-point. The two men were probably introduced by Dirck Coornhert, another of Cock's engravers. Both Ortelius and Coornhert were members of the 'Family of Love', a quasi-religious sect that skated on dangerously thin theological ice. Although conforming to the outward forms of the Catholic church, members of the Family believed that the individual should enjoy a personal relationship with God, without the mediation of the Church and without recourse to the traditional ceremonies of faith. They preached tolerance, humility and the avoidance of sin.

There is no conclusive evidence to prove that Bruegel was a member of this sect, but several features of his work betray a sympathy with its ideals. His disapproval of the excesses of both Protestantism and Catholicism was nowhere stressed more eloquently than in his late masterpiece, *The Parable of the Blind* (p.117), where the figure with the lute (a punning reference to Lutheranism) has already fallen in the ditch and is soon to be followed by a Catholic prominently displaying his trappings of a rosary and a crucifix.

MARRIAGE TO MAYKEN

In 1562, Bruegel visited Amsterdam, where he executed drawings of the city gates, and the following year he settled in Brussels with his new bride, Mayken, who was aged about 19. We know very little about Bruegel's wife; she was the daughter of his former master, Pieter Coecke, and Van Mander tells us that Bruegel 'often carried her about in his arms when she was a little girl'. Van Mander also informs us that the move to Brussels was forced on Bruegel by his mother-in-law, Mayken Verhulst Bessemers, because she wanted him to be firmly separated from a woman in Antwerp with whom he had had an earlier romantic entanglement.

Bernard Regent/Camerapix Hutchison Library

Niclaes Jonghelinck ordered a series of pictures depicting the months of the year. Only five of these now survive and despite the rapid brushwork and the thin paint surface, which suggest that Bruegel was working hurriedly, these rank among his finest achievements. *Hunters in the Snow* (p.126), in particular, with its masterly sense of space, became a model for future portrayals of winter scenes in the Low Countries.

Bruegel's stay in Brussels coincided with a period of immense political unrest and, not unnaturally, frequent attempts have been made to find some reflection of the Revolt of the Netherlands in the artist's works. However, Bruegel's art is essentially conservative in outlook and it must be remembered that he relied for much of his patronage upon important figures in the establishment. The much-despised Cardinal Granvelle was an ardent collector of his works, while Jonghelinck, who owned 16 of Bruegel's paintings, was a personal friend of Philip II and would have been equally sensitive, no doubt, to disapproval from official circles.

Many of the works which have been linked

A prosperous capital
In Bruegel's time, Brussels was a flourishing city of about 50,000 inhabitants. Its imposing buildings reflected its status as political capital of the Netherlands.

Whatever the reason for his move, it was a crucial one. Brussels presented him with new challenges and new opportunities, and in the last six years of his life there, Bruegel found his most important patrons and produced his greatest paintings. Where Antwerp had been a prosperous commercial centre, the spirit of his new home was both political and aristocratic. The Holy Roman Emperor Charles V had chosen the palace of the Dukes of Brabant for his ceremonial abdication in 1555 and his son Philip II, King of Spain, continued to use the city as his administrative base.

A CHANGE OF STYLE

It was in Brussels that some echoes of Italian trends finally found their way into Bruegel's art. Perhaps this was due to the example of Raphael's famous tapestry cartoons, which he could have seen there. These designs, among the most grandiose works of the High Renaissance, were sent to Brussels to serve as models for tapestries to be woven for the Sistine Chapel in Rome, and they had an enormous influence on Flemish artists. It is more probable, though, that Bruegel was meeting the demands of his new clientèle by producing work that was more in tune with current taste. He gradually abandoned his taste for panels crowded with incident, concentrating instead on single themes, using just a few, solidly-built figures.

Bruegel also recaptured his enthusiasm for landscape, which had seemingly been stifled during his time with Cock. In 1565, he received his largest commission, when the wealthy banker

A Dynasty of Painters

Bruegel's two sons were only infants when he died and they were reputedly taught painting by their grandmother, Mayken Verhulst Bessemers. Both sons spelled their name 'Brueghel', although their father had dropped the 'h' from his signature in about 1559. They both had painter sons, and further descendants carried on the family tradition until well in the 18th century, though without any great distinction.

Giraudon

'Hell Brueghel'
Pieter Brueghel the Younger (1564-1638) is best known for his copies and imitations of his father's peasant scenes, but he also painted scenes of Hell and fires, which earned him the nickname 'Hell Brueghel'. Like his brother Jan, he worked mainly in Antwerp.

A powerful patron
Cardinal Antoine de Granvelle, chief counsellor to Margaret of Austria, Philip II's regent in the Netherlands, owned several of Bruegel's paintings. He was a hated symbol of foreign oppression and the discontent he aroused was one of the causes of the revolt against Spanish rule. Granvelle himself did not witness the revolt as Philip, aware of his unpopularity, recalled him to Spain in 1564.

Lauros-Giraudon

Palais Granvelle, Besançon

with the atrocities of the Duke of Alva, Spanish governor of the Netherlands – *The Massacre of the Innocents* (p.127) for example – actually pre-date the events they are supposed to represent and it is only in his last paintings that some hint of the troubles can be detected.

In his final years, Bruegel returned to the depiction of proverbs, recasting them as monumental scenes of grand tragedy. The overriding mood was one of bleak pessimism. All the parties concerned were blinkered by fanaticism, complacency and self-interest. The blind were, indeed, leading the blind.

As has often been reflected in the aura surrounding many artists since, Bruegel's reputation increased enormously after his death in September 1569 and when, three years later, Cardinal Granvelle sought to replace the paintings he had lost during the rebellion, he found the prices prohibitive. Among painters, too, there was immense respect and it was fitting that when Jan Brueghel eventually chose a painting to adorn his parents' tomb, he selected a work by Rubens, one of Bruegel's greatest admirers and spiritual heir.

Giraudon

Musée des Beaux Arts, Strasbourg

'Velvet Brueghel'
Jan Brueghel (1568-1625) is known as 'Velvet Brueghel' because of his extraordinary skill in painting delicate textures. He specialized in flower paintings and lush landscapes, and often painted pieces in the work of other artists.

Witt Library

Bode Museum, East Berlin

A tribute from Rubens
Peter Paul Rubens, the greatest Flemish artist of the 17th century, painted this picture of Christ Giving the Keys to St Peter *that formerly adorned Bruegel's tomb in Notre Dame de la Chapelle, Brussels. Rubens was a great admirer of Bruegel and owned several paintings by him.*

The Ways of the World

**Throughout every stage of his career, Bruegel was a narrative painter,
using elaborate imagery and everyday incident to comment on
the human condition.**

Jean-Loup Charmet

Bruegel's greatness is so widely acknowledged today that it is hard to imagine that in his own time his supremacy was not recognized. He was immensely popular, but many contemporaries regarded his work as old-fashioned – mainly because Bruegel refused to be diverted by the innovations which his fellow-countrymen had been bringing into the Netherlands from Italy during the previous 50 years.

Bruegel's art was a development of older trends in neighbouring Flanders. More than a century earlier, the so-called 'Primitive' painters of Bruges had started depicting Biblical themes as scenes of contemporary life, with everyday objects used symbolically to underline the true meaning of the occasion. Bruegel favoured a similarly narrative approach but, in keeping with his cultured, humanist background, chose to depict secular rather than religious themes, emphasizing the follies of mankind rather than the rewards or punishments awaiting them in the next world.

Much of Bruegel's early imagery was inherited.

The Temptation of Saint Anthony
(above) Published in 1556, this is one of the earliest engravings of a Bruegel design. The subject is the popular legend of Saint Anthony stoically resisting the temptations and devilish lures sent to assail him. The imagery is a mixture of nightmarish creatures reminiscent of Bosch, traditional symbolism and proverbs. Hence the rotting fish and the one-eyed head symbolize the decay and corruption of the church and state.

Wedding Dance in the Open Air (1566)
(right) In later works Bruegel moves away from abstract symbolism, and shows man's vices in everyday terms. Here the dancers portray the sin of lust, for which the wedding is a pretext.

City of Detroit Purchase

The Detroit Institute of Art

Albertina, Vienna

The Artist and the Connoisseur (1566-68)

(above) This pen-and-ink drawing is a presumed self-portrait of the artist at work. His fierce concentration is highlighted by the fatuous expression of the unknown collector.

The Misanthrope (1568)

(right) A new pessimism is evident in Bruegel's last works. Here an old man mourns the faithless world, represented by the thief in the globe, while the blue coat symbolizes his own self-deceit.

Gallerie Nazionali di Capodimonte, Naples

Archiv für Kunst und Geschichte

From Bosch, there came a legacy of hellish creatures that derived ultimately from manuscript illuminations or the carved grotesques on choirstalls. To modern eyes, these may seem like visionary fantasies, but to a contemporary they could – quite literally – be read, like flamboyant hieroglyphics.

SOURCES OF INSPIRATION

However, Bruegel increasingly, drew inspiration from the strong undercurrent of popular literature that had developed since the introduction of printing. In the forefront of this tradition were the compilations of proverbs and moralizing anecdotes, taken from the Scriptures or the classics, which served effectively as laymen's Bibles.

By far the most influential of these collections was Sebastian Brant's *Ship of Fools*. First published in 1494, the book was still popular in Bruegel's day and, because of its numerous woodcut illustrations, made an enormous impression on contemporary artists. Brant's success spawned a host of similar works, not least the *Adages* of Erasmus, the celebrated Dutch humanist.

Bruegel reaped a rich harvest from sources such as these. Their influence is most obvious in works such as *Netherlandish Proverbs* (pp.122-3), where individual illustrations of human foolishness are colourfully and exhaustively catalogued. But it can

Colorphoto Hinz

also be seen in mythological and biblical paintings like *The Fall of Icarus* (pp.120-21) and *The Parable of the Blind* (p.117).

Other sources of visual inspiration were the festivities of the *rederijkkamer* or chambers of rhetoric, which organized processions with Christian or allegorical tableaux and outdoor performances of farces and morality plays. The spirit of these was captured in the panel *Carnival and Lent*, where the principal characters were

Two monkeys (1562)

(below) This painting of two chained monkeys is an unusual subject for Bruegel. It may be a comment on man's base nature. Through the arched window there is a distant view of the port of Antwerp.

Staatliche Museen Preussischer Kulturbesitz, Gemäldegalerie, Berlin (West)

embodied by satirical floats with their processions.

The vast majority of Bruegel's large scale paintings were executed on oak panels – a long-established tradition which required laborious preparation and a priming of size and gesso. During the early 16th century the gessoed panel gradually gave way to canvas, and oil began to replace tempera (ground pigments mixed with egg rather than oil). Bruegel's career occurred during a transitional stage in this development, and although most of his paintings are worked in oil on panel, he also painted in tempera on canvas. Only a handful of canvases have survived, the most notable being late works such as *The Parable of the Blind* and *The Misanthrope*.

A CHANGE IN STYLE

With his move to Brussels in 1563, Bruegel's work acquired a new eloquence. His new patrons there were not to be satisfied with densely-packed panels that were, in effect, outsize versions of prints. Gradually his paintings became less cluttered and the slight, semi-articulated figures of his early works were replaced with robust, corporeal peasants, full of individuality. This was due in the main to the dramatic improvements in his draughtsmanship, which seemed to be influenced by his increased study of Italian art.

The Parable of the Blind (1568)
(right and left) The theme of blindness recurs throughout Bruegel's work. Based on Matthew 15:14, *'And if the blind lead the blind, both shall fall into the ditch', this painting is a terrible image of fatality, not only of the blind men, but of all those who are blind to true religion – symbolized by the church in the background. Bruegel's acute powers of observation are apparent in the precise representation of different kinds of blindness, which have been identified. This man (left) is suffering from atrophy of the eyeball.*

COMPARISONS

Winter landscapes

The Flemish landscape tradition goes back to the early 1300s and the illustrated devotional manuals known as the Books of Hours. Bruegel drew on this tradition of his series of paintings depicting *The Months*, which included his memorable winter landscape *Hunters in the Snow* – one of the first large-scale pictures to deal with landscape and nature in its own right. Other winter village scenes anticipated the work of the 17th century Dutch painter Hendrick Avercamp.

National Gallery, London

Hendrick Avercamp (1585-1634) Winter Scene, Skaters
(left) This deaf and dumb painter specialized in delicate winter scenes. Colourful figures skating on a frozen lake create a vivid impression of a cold winter's day.

The Limbourg brothers (died c.1416) Les Très Riches Heures du Duc de Berri: February
(right) This Book of Hours is illustrated by appropriate scenes from contemporary life.

Giraudon

Musée Condé, Chantilly

Gallerie Nazionali di Capodimonte, Naples

More important were the series of *naer het leven* (from life) drawings, which date from this period. These masterly studies of peasants, soldiers and tradesmen reveal a new conviction in their strength of line and appreciation of volume. Carefully finished in chalk, pen and ink, their detail suggests they were finished in the studio; even so, they demonstrate that Bruegel was taking a direct interest in human subjects, rather than just working from print sources.

TRIPS INTO THE COUNTRY

Van Mander related the story of how Bruegel and a friend called Hans Franckert used to disguise themselves as peasants and steal into the countryside to observe rustic weddings and fairs unseen. The tale may well be apocryphal, but was probably suggested by sketches such as these. Certainly, it was in Bruegel's later paintings that his figure studies paid their greatest dividends.

In works like *The Peasant Dance* (p.131), for example, he achieved his most successful synthesis of naturalism and lay preaching. At first glance, the picture may seem like a faithful portrayal of harmless merry-making, but in fact it is a reworking of an old theme: man's sins and the neglect of religion. The church and the shrine on the right lie abandoned, the leading dancer steps blindly on a cross of straw, and symbols of most of the vices, including adultery, are readily apparent. As a naturistically presented piece of moralizing, this set an example for the Dutch genre painters of succeeding generations.

TRADEMARKS
Hidden faces

Bruegel was far more concerned with characterizing human types than with portraying particular individuals. He often used hats and head-dresses to obscure faces, revealing character through the figure as a whole.

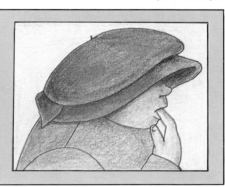

Studies from life
(left) During the 1560s Bruegel made numerous sketches of peasants and townspeople. Although none of them can be identified as models for figures in his paintings, the detailed notes which accompany many of them suggest that they may have been used to reinforce his memory when painting clothing and equipment.

Albertina, Vienna

117

THE MAKING OF A MASTERPIECE

Netherlandish Proverbs

Proverbs and figures of speech were popular subjects for illustration in Bruegel's time, and a constant theme in his own work. Nowhere are they treated in such an obvious or encyclopedic way as in this painting, where a whole village acts out over 100 different adages and expressions (some of which are translated here). These fall into two groups – those which show the absurdity of human behaviour, such as the figure carrying baskets of light into the sunshine (5), and those which demonstrate sinfulness, such as the woman wrapping a blue cloak around her husband, symbolizing her adultery. Bruegel may have modelled the painting on a contemporary engraving by Frans Hogenberg, which bears the inscription 'This is generally called the Blue Cloak, but it would be better named The World's Follies'. This alternative title could equally well be applied to Bruegel's work, which is essentially an instructive commentary on the ridiculous spectacle of human life.

1 The sow removes the spigot

To make a pig of oneself

2 He butts his head against the wall

To bang one's head against a brick wall

3 Don't count your chickens before they hatch

4 He speaks out of two mouths
To be two-faced

5 He carries baskets of light into the sunshine
To sell ice-cubes to Eskimos

6 One holds the distaff while the other spins
It takes two to gossip

The Blue Cloak
(*above*) This engraving by
Frans Hogenberg was
probably the immediate
source for Bruegel's
painting, which was
known by the same name
for many years. Bruegel
replaced the abstract
landscape with a realistic
village setting and
increased the number of
proverbs from 40 to over a
hundred.

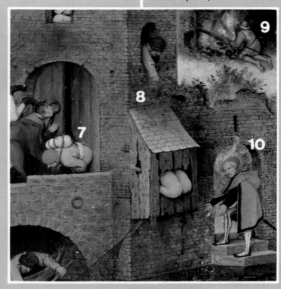

7 He opens the door with his bottom
He doesn't know whether he's coming or going

8 He kills two flies with one blow
To kill two birds with one stone

9 He doesn't care whose house is burning as long
as he can warm himself from the coals
Every man for himself

10 He throws money into the water
To throw money down the drain

11 To poke a stick into the wheel
To put a spoke in the wheel/throw a curve

12 He who spills his gruel can't pick it all up
It's no use crying over spilt milk

13 He cannot reach from one loaf to the other
He cannot make ends meet

14 They pull for the long piece
To draw straws/pull the wishbone

Bruegel painted in an age when art served a moral purpose and his narrative paintings reflect this tradition. The Fall of Icarus is Bruegel's only work with a mythological subject. Like Netherlandish Proverbs, it symbolizes the follies of mankind.

The Haymakers, The Corn Harvest and Hunters in the Snow are probably his most

celebrated works. These panoramic landscapes depict the months of the year in terms of man's relationship with nature.

The Massacre of the Innocents is one of a number of winter scenes with religious themes. As in his previous works, the artist looks down on the tiny figures from above. A biblical story also forms the basis of The Conversion of St Paul, but this time a low viewpoint is adopted. A similar angle is also used in The Wedding Feast and The Peasant Dance, where it is accompanied by a striking change in scale. The figures here are shown close-up, with a new monumentality that gives these paintings of peasant life a particular immediacy and vigour.

The Fall of Icarus *c.1558-66*
29″ × 44″ Musée Royaux des Beaux-Arts, Brussels

The theme of this idyllic painting is the mythological tale of Icarus, who fell to his death after flying too close to the sun. Bruegel transforms the legend by showing Icarus after he has fallen into the sea (only his legs are visible) and the ploughman, the shepherd and the fisherman work on, oblivious to his fate. An eloquent portrayal of the futility of ambition, the work also shows man's blindness to the world.

121

Netherlandish Proverbs *1559*
46″ × 64″ Staatliche Museen, Berlin

Also called The Blue Cloak *after the central figure of the adulterous woman who is wrapping a cloak of deceit round her husband, this painting depicts over 100 proverbs and sayings. The absurd activities of the villagers reflect the topsy-turvy nature of the world, symbolized by the inverted globe on the house in the left of the picture. Many images, such as the blind men on the horizon and the man in the crystal globe, also appear in other works.*

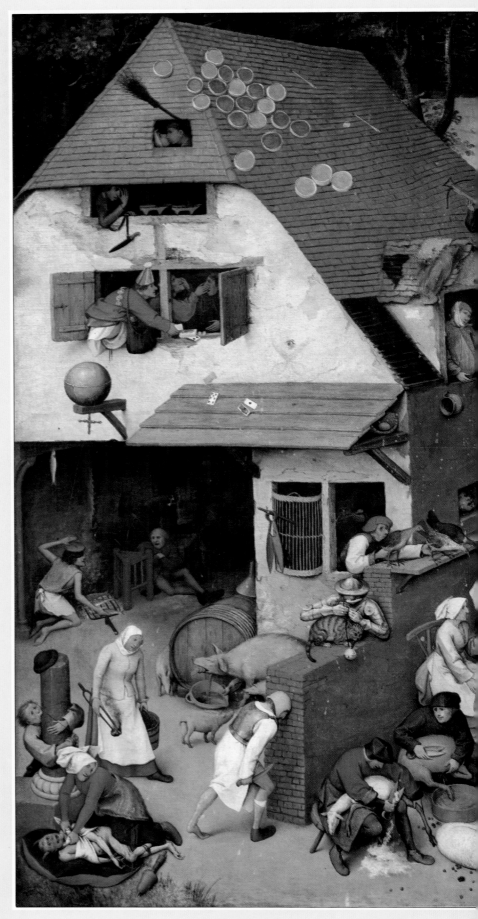

Haymaking 1565
46" × 63½" National Gallery, Prague

One of a series of five pictures depicting The Months, this magnificent painting is thought to represent July.
The tranquil landscape pulses with the activity of haymakers and fruit harvesters hard at work.

The Corn Harvest 1565
46½″ × 63¼″ Metropolitan Museum of Art, New York

This vast, sultry landscape, dominated by a golden harvest, is thought to depict the month of August. The path through the corn leads the eye to the field hands pausing for a mid-day meal in the shade of a tree.

Hunters in the Snow 1565
46″ × 63¾″ Kunsthistorisches Museum, Vienna

This bleak winter landscape is possibly the most famous of all Bruegel's works and probably depicts the month of January. The sense of space and depth is emphasized by the bold shapes in the foreground.

Massacre of the Innocents c.1566
45¾" × 63" Kunsthistorisches Museum, Vienna

One of several paintings where a biblical theme is treated in a contemporary way, this winter's scene highlights the atrocities of Herod's soldiers, shown as a Spanish punitive force attacking a Flemish village.

The Conversion of St Paul *1567*
42½″ × 61½″ Kunsthistorisches Museum,
Vienna

*This biblical story is set in a magnificent
mountain landscape, which must have been
inspired by Bruegel's journey through the
Alps. Seen through the eyes of a foot-soldier,
the principal event is obscured and reduced to
a tiny detail at the centre of the composition.
The work may be an allusion to the Duke of
Alva's crossing of the Alps in 1567, but it can
also be interpreted as being symbolic of man's
strivings to find true faith.*

Bridgeman Art Library

The Wedding Feast c.1568
44¾" × 64" Kunsthistorisches Museum, Vienna

The festive atmosphere and contemporary customs of a peasant wedding feast are superbly captured in this well-known painting. The strong emphasis on food and drink suggest that it may also be an illustration of gluttony.

The Peasant Dance c.1568
44¾" × 64½" Kunsthistorisches Museum, Vienna

One of Bruegel's liveliest peasant scenes, this painting shows the celebration of a kermess or Saint's day. The underlying theme is one of religious neglect, and signs of, lust, anger and gluttony are all apparent.

131

Peasant Life

The Netherlandish peasants of Bruegel's day had a harsh but relatively prosperous existence. While they toiled endlessly for small reward, they celebrated and feasted on a lavish scale.

Drinking companions
(below) Community life revolved around the church and the tavern, which were usually at the heart of the village. In their spare time, the peasants strolled to the inn, where they drank great quantities of cheap ale and played cards or skittles. Tea-drinking was not introduced until the late 17th century, so the tavern was still the best place to get a refreshing drink and mix with your neighbours.

In 1500 the Dutch scholar Erasmus fondly described his fellow countrymen as having 'a straightforward nature, without treachery or deceit, and not prone to any serious vices, except that it is a little given to pleasure, especially of feasting'. He attributed this to 'the wonderful supply of everything which can tempt them to enjoyment', due largely to the wealth and fertility of the region. Bruegel's paintings of peasants carousing at carnival time or celebrating another fruitful harvest, reflect this lighter aspect of peasant life.

A VIOLENT AGE

Erasmus could have used the same words to describe the inhabitants of other provinces in the Low Countries – particularly Flanders and Brabant. By contemporary West-European standards, many people were indeed prosperous and well-fed, living off a lush, fertile land. But, as

Riotous feasting
(right) The peasants seized any opportunity for merrymaking. Indeed, wedding feasts attracted so many villagers, that in 1546 an Imperial decree was issued, limiting the guests to 20.

Bildarchiv Preussische Kulturbesitz/Photo: Braun

Bruegel also revealed in his pictures just 50 years later, there was another, darker side to their lives. The poor and sick generally had to fend for themselves, and violence was never far away. This was a time when the torture, execution and mutilation of criminals provided mass entertainment; when attacks by bandits and marauding soldiers were a constant threat; and when a drunken peasant would not think twice before reaching for his knife in a brawl.

In the Low Countries, few people lived far from a town – in fact, in Flanders and Brabant almost two-thirds of the population lived in towns. But the peasants' world rarely extended beyond their village and the surrounding fields. Everything they knew about the large urban centres such as Antwerp, Amsterdam and Bruges was learnt from the Catholic village priest or the travelling entertainers, merchants and small traders who occasionally passed by.

THE RURAL COMMUNITY

Villages were small – few had more than 200 to 600 inhabitants – and people lived, together with their livestock, in small thatched huts made of wood and mud. In the centre of each village was the parish church and, often, a tavern. A little apart from the rest of the buildings stood the lord's manor house.

The lord owned all the surrounding land but the better-off peasants had the customary right to lease and till a share of it. In return, they had to give the lord some of their produce and perhaps work on his 'demesne' – the area which the lord kept for himself. The less fortunate peasants had

Tavern Scene/David Teniers

Pieter Brueghel the Younger/Peasant Wedding/Pommersfelden Castle

The casualties of war
(right) Following the
Duke of Alva's invasion of
the Netherlands in 1567,
the peasants were
constantly at risk from
marauding soldiers and
mercenaries. There was
wide-scale looting and
violence, and the village
granaries were continually
being emptied.

Atlas van Stolk

Van Uden and Teniers II/Peasants merrymaking before a country house/National Gallery, London

no customary rights to arable land and either they
leased it on an annual basis or they hired out their
services to others. All peasants usually had the
right to graze their animals on the common
pasture or the village's area of wasteland.

The arable land was not divided into small
fields surrounded by hedges and fences, but into
narrow strips barely wide enough for an oxen or
horse-drawn plough. Traditionally, each peasant
had a number of such strips, not together but
scattered far and wide, on a mixture of fertile and

Fotomas Index

infertile land. In much of Western Europe, the
strips were divided among three fields, one of
which was left fallow while the other two were
used for growing wheat, rye, barley, millet and
oats – crops which were needed as much for the
brewing of beer as for the making of bread.
However, the disadvantages of the inefficient
three-field system had been recognized by the
wealthier peasants of the Low Countries long
before the 16th century. Many had acquired the
right to farm adjoining strips and they now grew
an increasing variety of crops.

ADVANCED FARMING

They grew hemp and flax and plants which
provided dyes, such as woad, for the cloth-making
industry. The linen industry in particular was
beginning to flourish in Brabant, where it provided
peasants with a means of supplementing their
income by spinning or weaving in the home. The
more enterprising farmers also grew hops for beer,
turnips, peas and beans and they adopted the
practice – advanced for the times – of spreading

The lord's domain
(above) The lord's manor
stood a little apart from
the rest of the village, in
its own extensive grounds.
The peasants' relationship
with the gentleman
landowners was, on the
whole, amicable, as long
as they were granted a
degree of self-sufficiency
and their routine remained
unchanged.

Prey to tax-collectors
(left) The peasants paid
heavy taxes to the state, as
well as rents and tithes to
the lord and the church.
All in all, between 20 and
40 per cent of their produce
was consumed in this way.

Two Tax Gatherers/Marinus van Reymerswaele/National Gallery, London

manure on the fields.

The harvesting of the crops was an activity in which all the community joined in. The men cut the corn while the women gathered it up and carried it to waiting wagons. The whole community also helped to harvest hay and gather fruit and nuts, which were in plentiful supply in the Low Countries. Many kinds of fruit are grown', wrote an Italian resident, but 'except for many varieties of pears and apples which are excellent . . . the fruits lack the fragrance and flavour that they possess in Italy'.

GREEN PASTURES

In Holland, dairy cattle grazing in lush pastures were a familiar sight. Holland had once been an impoverished region of bogs and marshes, but by organizing themselves into district committees the more wealthy peasants had managed to transform the landscape. With the help of watermills, sluices and dikes they had created a fertile land of pastures and arable fields. The oxen were huge and produced an enormous amount of milk, while

Harvest time
(below) In August, the whole community participated in the harvest – the most important event of the agricultural year. The men scythed the corn while the women gathered it into bundles, carrying it on their backs to horse-drawn wagons. If the harvest was bad, the peasants went hungry for the following year.

Colorphoto Hinz/Basel

Fine Art Photographic Library Limited

Pieter Bruegel the Elder/The Harvest

the horses were large, heavy-headed animals, ideal for agricultural tasks.

Life was governed by the seasons, and the calendar was still seen in terms of each month's rural activity. August, for instance, was harvest time, while in February the peasants gathered wood for their fires. Summer, according to the Italian resident, was delightful 'because the heat is usually not too severe and flies and gnats do not get in the nose very much'. Winter, however, was invariably 'long and stormy' and the coastland was racked by gales. It was a hard life, and the average life expectancy was only 30 to 35 years. Up to 50 per cent of children died in their first year, and those who survived were expected to assume an adult role from a very early age. They were dressed in adult clothing and sent into the fields.

THE THREAT OF DISASTER

For most peasants, there was not only the fear of death – the communities were riddled with disease – but also famine. An excessively cold or wet spell could wipe out a year's crop – indeed, 1566 became known as a 'Year of Hunger'. And if the weather was kind, there was always the danger that their crops would be seized by bandits or soldiers from France or Spain. These two countries treated Flanders as their primary battleground in their struggle for supremacy. Even after the signing of a peace treaty in 1559 there was little respite, for Philip of Spain was determined to rule the Low Countries with an iron hand.

Living as they did under the constant threat of disaster, the peasants felt that they were at the mercy of supernatural powers. Every setback was considered to be the work of demons, witches, werewolves and the spirits of the dead, all of whom had to be appeased through spiritual acts.

Market day

(left) When the grain had been harvested it was distributed among the peasants – but only after the lord and the church had claimed their portion. The peasants then sold their produce in the village market-place, filling large baskets with bread and giant kegs with beer.

Holy feast days

(below) The peasants always kept holy festivals, including the feast of St Nicholas Eve (5 December). As St Nicholas was the patron saint of children, the young ones were given baskets and stockings filled with gifts.

Fools and quackery

(left) 'Witches' and healers played on the ignorance and superstition of the peasants (often in open competition with the clergy). This engraving by Bruegel shows a man being cured of a brain tumour: the old woman holds a stone up which she has supposedly cut out of his head.

Pieter Brueghel the Younger/The Village Market

Pieter Bruegel the Elder/The Witch of Malleghem (detail)

Atlas von Stolk

The Church, of course, represented the greatest power of all and had an enormous hold over the peasants in both their spiritual and daily life. Each year it collected tithes which mounted to about 10 per cent of everything they produced. It also provided them with days of rest, or holy days, when occasions such as the Assumption of the Virgin or the Feast of the Circumcision were celebrated. In cities like Antwerp, the celebrations took the form of huge processions in which the religious orders, craftsmen and merchants marched to the music of pipes and drums. There were floats on which scenes from the New Testament were enacted or boys and girls stood dressed in the robes of saints.

OCCASIONS FOR FEASTING

In the villages, the holy day celebrations were a much quieter affair. The festivals which the peasants most looked forward to were determined by the seasons and the agricultural cycle. The summer solstice (24-29 June) was a particularly riotous occasion, when the malevolent spirits were expelled. And provided the harvest was good, there was always a big celebration in early November, at the beginning of a period of enforced idleness. This was the time when the granaries were full and the animals which could not be kept through the winter were slaughtered, salted and smoked. There would be feasting, music and dancing, and liberal quantities of beer would be consumed. For a few hours at least, the peasants could forget their hard daily life.

The winter

(left) In winter, the land could not be worked so the peasants hunted for food, gathered wood for their fires, or amused themselves by skating on the frozen lakes.

The Fotomas Index

Dirk Dalens/Dordrecht – Zierikzee

135

A Year in the Life 1567

It was a year of bloody religious conflict. The massed troops of Imperial Spain poured into the Netherlands as Philip II strove to enforce the Inquisition. Catholic fought Protestant in a civil war in France. And one night in Scotland, the Catholic husband of Queen Mary was strangled by an unknown hand.

In July of the summer of 1567, a force of 60,000 infantry and 12,000 cavalry swept into the Netherlands under the command of the Duke of Alva, Fernando Alvarez de Toledo. A revolt had broken out in Bruegel's homeland, then the northernmost part of the Spanish Empire, and Alva had been sent to crush it.

The storm had been brewing throughout the 1560s in this prosperous outpost of the empire, where Philip II's exorbitant taxes had aroused deep resentment among the rich burgers of the cities. As the traditional ruling classes of the Netherlands attempted to regain control from their Spanish overlords, an influx of Protestant ideas from France was fomenting religious discontent. And to add fuel to the fire, the 'hunger winter' of 1566 brought starvation to many of the poor.

Philip was determined to stamp out the revolt. He was

Florence's new bridge
From 1567-69 the elegant new bridge of Santa Trinità was built across the river Arno in Florence. It was designed by the Mannerist sculptor and architect Bartolommeo Ammanati.

Alva's reign of terror
(left) In the 1560s, Protestants in the Netherlands revolted against their Spanish Catholic overlords. Dismayed at the ineffectiveness of the Inquisition in this northern corner of his Empire, Philip II sent in his troops in 1567 – under the command of Fernando Alvarez de Toledo, the Duke of Alva. This painting shows him presiding over his judicial court: the bloody execution of dissidents in the background illustrates the probable future of those kneeling before him.

particularly disturbed by the news of religious dissent in the Netherlands and the ineffectiveness of the Inquisition there. The rise of Calvinism – an extreme form of Protestantism – was reported back to Madrid in alarming terms. A fervent Catholic himself, Philip was convinced that bloody repression was not merely the sole solution, but was also completely justified.

A CRUSHING DEFEAT

Some advisers felt that Philip himself should lead the invasion force, but most argued that the risk of assassination was too great. Command went to Alva instead, but the army – marching from Italy – could not set out until spring 1567, when the snow had melted from the Alpine passes. Meanwhile,

Spanish troops already stationed in the Netherlands were reinforced with troops battle-hardened from years of war against the Turks. In March, a crack force of 800 swiftly crushed the main rebel army of 3,000 'raw levies, untrained vagabond's and thieves' at Oosterweel. But the ferocity of the repression merely strengthened Dutch resolve, and their hatred of the Spanish invaders.

The main army under Alva arrived in mid summer. Iron discipline had been maintained during the long march north, with any soldier who tempted a woman's virtue certain to find himself hanging from the nearest tree. Alva applied the same merciless principles to the Dutch dissidents in Brussels. On his arrival on 9 August he swiftly arrested two of the leading rebels, Count Egmont and Count Horn – both were executed for

The battle of St Denis
(above) A civil war was raging in France between the ruling Catholics and the Protestant (Huguenot) rebels. On 10 November 1567, Louis de Bourbon, Prince de Condé, led his Huguenot army in an unsuccessful attempt to defeat the government troops at the Battle of St Denis in Paris. Condé withdrew from the capital, and travelled south to besiege the town of Chartres.

Akbar's Indian Empire
(right) In 1567, the Mogul Emperor Akbar the Great conquered the Indian province of Chitor, making it part of his growing empire which eventually stretched right across northern India. Art, architecture and literature all flourished under Akbar's stable and tolerant rule: this manuscript illumination shows the emperor and his entourage on a hunting expedition.

treason the following year. And Alva quickly established a judicial tribunal, the notorious Council of Troubles, to try all cases of heresy and subversion. The Council, which put thousands to death, earned the name 'the council of blood'; but Philip felt no remorse, describing the dissidents as 'vile animals'.

EUROPE IN TURMOIL

The crisis in the Netherlands was part of a wider pattern of religious upheaval throughout Europe. In France, 1567 witnessed the outbreak of the second of three civil wars fought between Catholics and Huguenots during the decade. These struggles culminated in the St Bartholomew's Eve Massacre of August 1572, when 3,000 Huguenots were killed in Paris and 10,000 in provincial towns in four days of carnage.

In Britain, Elizabeth I feared constantly for her own life at the hands of Catholic extremists. But the most sensational murder of the year was of a Catholic: Lord Henry Darnley, the 22-year-old syphilitic husband of Mary, Queen of Scots, was strangled, reputedly on the instructions of the Earl of Bothwell. The Queen did not grieve for long – if at all. Before the year's end, she was married again, this time to Bothwell.

Britain herself would soon be drawn into the maelstrom of the Netherlands, where the political terror of the Duke of Alva would in the long run prove a complete failure. No reconciliation would ever be achieved between Spain and the Low Countries – indeed 1567 saw the beginning of what the Dutch now call 'The Eighty Years War'.

A murder and a marriage
(right and below) On the night of 10 February 1567, Lord Henry Darnley, the scheming and unpopular husband of Mary Queen of Scots was staying at the remote house of 'Kirk O' Fields' in Edinburgh, while the queen (conveniently) attended a servant's wedding. Some time during the night, the house was blown up, and the next morning Darnley's strangled corpse was discovered in the garden. The murder was reputedly arranged by the Earl of Bothwell, whom Mary (below) later married.

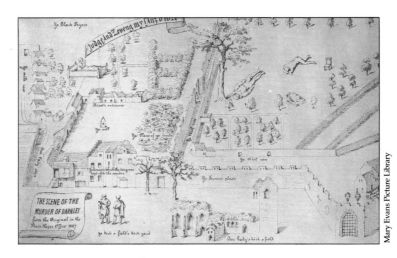

The founding of Rio de Janeiro
(below) Dominated by the spectacular Sugar Loaf Mountain, the Brazilian capital of Rio – or Sao Sebastiao do Rio de Janeiro – was founded in 1567. Both the Portugese and the French had made temporary settlements in the area before the 1560s, but in 1567, a Portugese expedition lead by Mem de Sá defeated the French colonists, and moved the existing Portugese settlement to a permanent site on the hill known as the Morro do Castelo.

GALLERY GUIDE

Dürer

Most of Dürer's paintings are still in Germany. The best collection is in the Alte Pinakothek in Munich, though there are several paintings also in the Germanisches Nationalmuseum in Dürer's native Nuremberg. American galleries possess few important examples; the most interesting is undoubtedly a double-sided panel in the National Gallery in Washington. British and American collections are in a much happier position with Dürer's graphic work. The British Museum in London has one of the finest collections of his drawings and prints, and American museums with good representations include the Metropolitan Museum of Art in New York and the Fogg Art Museum in Cambridge, Massachusetts.

Cranach

Cranach was extremely prolific, and paintings by him or from his studio are in many galleries throughout the world. The majority, however, are still in collections in Germany and in German-speaking countries. Among the museums with the richest collections of his work are the Gemäldegalerie in Dresden, the Alte Pinakothek in Munich and the Kunsthistorisches Museum in Vienna. In the USA, the best collections are in the Metropolitan Museum of Art in New York, including one of his many paintings of *The Judgement of Paris* (p.54-5), and the National Gallery of Art in Washington.

Holbein

Holbein is one of the very few major German artists whose work is best represented outside his native country. In the German-speaking world, the best collection of his work is in the Öffentliche Kunstsammlung in Basel in Switzerland, where Holbein spent much of his early career. In Britain, the collection of his drawings in the Royal Library at Windsor Castle is unrivalled and there are also several paintings in the royal collection, which are usually on show at Hampton Court or sometimes in temporary exhibitions at the Queen's Gallery in London. Elsewhere in Britain, Holbein is principally represented in the National Gallery and the National Portrait Gallery in London. In the USA, Holbein is particularly well represented in New York; the Metropolitan Museum of Art has several portraits (p.83) and the Frick Collection has outstanding portraits of two of the major political figures of Henry VIII's reign – Thomas More (p.92) and Thomas Cromwell. Other American museums with paintings by Holbein include the St Louis Art Museum (p.91) and the Museum of Art, Toledo, Ohio (p.99).

Bruegel

Bruegel's surviving output as a painter is small – only about 50 pictures are generally accepted as his. Of these, almost a third are in the superb collection of his work in the Kunsthistorisches Museum in Vienna. Otherwise, Bruegel is best represented in the Musées Royaux des Beaux-Arts in Brussels, which has *The Fall of Icarus* (pp.120-21) and several other pictures. Among the few Bruegel paintings in America, the oustanding works are *The Corn Harvest* in the Metropolitan Museum of Art, New York (p.125), and *Wedding Dance in the Open Air* in the Detroit Institute of Art (p.114). Bruegel's drawings, though more numerous than his paintings, are fairly rare. The best collection is in the Albertina in Vienna.

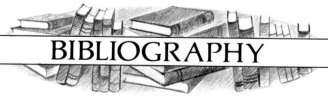

BIBLIOGRAPHY

C. Cuttler, *Northern Painting from Pucelle to Bruegel*, Holt, Rinehart and Winston, New York, 1968
P. Ganz, *The Paintings of Hans Holbein*, Phaidon, London, 1950
W. Gibson, *Bruegel*, Thames & Hudson, New York, 1985
C. Gilbert, *History of Renaissance Art throughout Europe*, Abrams, New York, 1972
R. Hughes and P. Bianconi, *The Complete Paintings of Bruegel*, Abrams, New York, 1969
W. Kurth, *The Complete Woodcuts of Albrecht Dürer*, Dover, New York, 1963

M. Levey, *Dürer*, Norton, New York, 1964
G. von der Osten and H. Vey, *Painting and Sculpture in Germany and the Netherlands 1500-1600*, Penguin Books, Baltimore, 1969
K. Parker, *Holbein's Drawings at Windsor Castle*, Johnson Reprint Corp., New York, 1983
J. Roberts, *Holbein*, Hippocrene Books, New York, 1980
A. Smith and A. Ottina della Chiesa, *The Complete Paintings of Dürer*, Abrams, New York, 1968
W. Strauss, *The Complete Engravings, Etchings and Drypoints of Albrecht Dürer*, Dover, New York, 1972

OTHER NORTHERN RENAISSANCE ARTISTS

Albrecht Altdorfer, (c.1480-1538)

German painter and printmaker, one of the most original of Dürer's contemporaries. He worked in Regensburg and was city architect there, although no architectural works by him are known. Most of his pictures are religious works, but he is renowned particularly for his great contribution to the development of landscape painting, for he was perhaps the first artist to paint 'pure' landscapes without any figures at all (an example is in the National Gallery, London). The term 'Danube School' is sometimes applied to German artists of this time who showed such a pioneering interest in landscape, and Lucas Cranach himself (in his early work) comes within the meaning of the term.

Hans Baldung Grien, (1484/5-1545)

German painter, graphic artist and designer. He worked mainly in Strasbourg, but he probably trained with Dürer in Nuremberg. His output was both varied and extensive, including paintings on various subjects (religious, historical, mythological, allegorical and portraits), designs for tapestries and stained glass, and numerous book illustrations. Something of Dürer's influence is seen in Baldung's nudes, which are often Italianate in flavour, but the sense of the mysterious and macabre that permeated his work was thoroughly in the northern tradition. His most characteristic works are small erotic allegories.

Jerome Cock, (1510-70)

Netherlandish engraver and publisher, the son of a painter called Jan de Cock. He worked mainly in Antwerp, but he visited Italy and played an influential role in promoting the work of other artists who had been there. Cock published prints of their work and also of that of Italian artists such as Raphael. Bruegel worked much for him in his early career.

Pieter Coecke van Aelst, (1502-50)

Netherlandish painter, designer and publisher, Bruegel's father-in-law. In his day he was regarded as one of the leading painters in Antwerp, but his paintings are now considered run-of-the-mill and he is remembered mainly for his publishing activities, which helped to spread Renaissance ideas in northern Europe. In the early 1520s he spent some time in Rome, and in 1533 he visited Constantinople on a mission to gain work there for the famous tapestry works in Brussels. In this he was unsuccessful, but he made some fascinating drawings on his journey that were published by his widow Mayken Verhulst (Bruegel's mother-in-law) in a book entitled The Manners and Customs of the Turks (1553).

Frans Floris, (c.1516-70)

Netherlandish painter, one of the most important exponents of the 'Romanist' style in Flanders. He worked in Italy in the early 1540s, and he was present in Rome in 1541 at the unveiling of Michelangelo's Last Judgement in the Sistine Chapel, a work that made an overwhelming impact on him. After his return to his native Antwerp in 1547 he acquired a great reputation with religious and historical works full of vigorous Michelangelesque nudes. According to his contemporary biographer Karel van Mander, he was immensely popular as a teacher, but in spite of his success he died in poverty as a result of his extravagant lifestyle.

Jan Gossaert, (c.1478-1533)

Netherlandish painter, also known as Mabuse. He was a widely travelled and influential figure, important in spreading Italianate motifs in northern Europe. He was in Italy himself in 1508 and the visit transformed his style. The Italian artist and biographer Giorgio Vasari praised him as 'almost the first to take to Flanders from Italy the true method of making scenes full of nude figures and poetical fancies', but his nudes actually seem to be more directly influenced by Albrecht Dürer's work than by Italian models.

Mathis Grünewald, (c.1470/80-1528)

German painter. He was the greatest German contemporary of Dürer, but is opposite in almost every way. His paintings are exclusively on religious themes and he had none of Dürer's wide-ranging visual curiosity, concentrating instead on expressing extreme emotional intensity. He made the subject of the Crucifixion his own, and his most celebrated depiction of it – the central panel of the great altarpiece for the abbey at Isenheim in Alsace (now in the Musée d'Unterlinden at Colmar) – is one of the most awe-inspiring paintings in the history of art. He understood Renaissance ideas of perspective, but spiritually he belongs entirely to the late-medieval world. Grünewald contrasts greatly with Dürer in his posthumous fame as well as in the character of his work. Whereas Dürer is one of only a very few artists whose reputation has always stood at the highest level, Grünewald was virtually forgotten until rediscovered in the early 20th century.

Maerten van Heemskerck, (1498-1574)

Netherlandish painter, active mainly in Haarlem, which is near to Heemskerck, the village of his birth. In 1532-5 he was in Italy, where he made numerous drawings of ancient buildings and statuary that are extremely valuable as evidence of contemporary knowledge of the remains of classical antiquity. Among his other works done in Rome is a splendid self-portrait (1533, Fitzwilliam Museum, Cambridge) in which he shows himself in front of the Colosseum. Heemskerck was much influenced by Michelangelo as well as by the antique, and his religious paintings are often notable for their vigorous depiction of the nude. His work was much engraved and was highly influential in spreading the Italianate style in the Netherlands.

John and Frances Croker (c.1580-85)
(above) This double portrait was painted by Nicholas Hilliard, limner to Queen Elizabeth I. Limning – miniature-painting – was regarded as an aristocratic art until, in 1579, Hilliard opened a workshop in Gutter Lane, London.

Bridgeman Art Library

140

Nicholas Hilliard (1547-1619)

The greatest English-born painter of the 16th century. Son of a goldsmith and trained as such, Hilliard was painting miniatures by 1560. In 1570 he painted his first dated portrait of Queen Elizabeth I, whose limner and goldsmith he already was. Between 1576 and 1578 he was in France and may have been attached to the suite of the Duc d'Alençon, the Queen's suitor. In his treatise The Arte of Limning (written about 1600) Hilliard mentions conversations with the Queen in which they agreed that portrait painting should be done without shadows, in a manner derived from Holbein. In his miniatures he carefully recorded all the contemporary elaborate costumes and jewels – in fact, Hilliard's works should be thought of as jewels, with exquisite cases and calligraphic inscription which he also created.

Lucas van Leyden (1494-1533)

Netherlandish engraver and painter, active mainly in his native Leyden. With Dürer he ranks as one of the supreme figures in the history of engraving and he was also one of the outstanding Netherlandish painters of his period. He was extremely precocious and produced a large body of work, even though he died fairly young; this makes it hard to credit the story told by his early biographer Karel van Mander that he was a dilettante and sometimes worked in bed. In 1521 Lucas met Dürer in Antwerp and he was profoundly influenced by the great German artist's work.

Quentin Massys (1465/6-1530)

Netherlandish painter. He worked mainly in Antwerp, where he was the leading painter of his day. His work continues the tradition of the great Netherlandish artists of the 15th century, but he was also influenced by Renaissance art and may well have visited Italy during his early career, which is poorly documented. He painted religious and genre scenes and was a distinguished portraitist, pioneering a new type of portrait showing a scholar in his study, as in his well-known picture of Erasmus (Galleria Nazionale, Rome).

Michael Pacher, (active 1465?-98)

Austrian painter and sculptor. He worked mainly at Bruneck in the Tyrol and was one of the first artists in the German-speaking countries to show distinct influence from the Italian Renaissance in his work. His sculpture (he was a virtuoso woodcarver) remained in the intricate late-Gothic tradition, but in his painting he comes close in spirit to the work of Mantegna, particularly in the way he uses low viewpoints to dramatic effect and sets his figures very close to the spectator. The difference is clearly seen in his greatest work, the St Wolfgang Altar in the church of St Wolfgang on the Abersee, a huge work incorporating both painting and sculpture. Although there is no documentary evidence that Pacher ever visited Italy, it is close to the Tyrol and it is very likely that he did at some time go there.

Martin Schongauer, (c.1430-91)

German engraver and painter, active in Colmar in Alsace. He was the greatest engraver of the generation before Dürer and had an enormous contemporary reputation – Dürer hoped to study with him, but Schongauer died before he reached Colmar. Schongauer holds a position of the highest importance in the history of engraving, for he brought a new richness and maturity to the medium. Before him, engraving had been primarily an offshoot of the goldsmith's art, but Schongauer gave it a much more painterly quality by expanding its range of tones and textures.

Jan van Scorel, (1495-1562)

Netherlandish painter, active mainly in Utrecht. Between 1519 and 1524 he made a long journey during which he visited several German towns, the islands of Crete, Cyprus and Rhodes, Jerusalem and Italy. In Rome he was given a prestigious appointment by Pope Hadrian VI, who was a native of Utrecht, and on his return to his country he immediately became a leader in the artistic world. Unlike many northern artists who travelled south, Scorel absorbed much more than the superficial characteristics of Italian art; his work has a sense of classical dignity and proportion that shows his understanding went much deeper. He was the first artist to bring a mature understanding of the ideals of the Renaissance to the area now called Holland and his work had great influence, his pupils including Maerten van Heemskerck. Scorel excelled as both a religious painter and a portraitist.

Michael Wolgemut, (1434-1519)

German engraver and painter, active in his native Nuremberg. In 1472 Wolgemut married the widow of his former teacher Hans Pleydenwurff, took over his flourishing shop and became the most important book illustrator in the city. He made considerable advances in the use of woodcuts as book illustrations, achieving a more harmonious integration of pictures and text than had previously been achieved and refining the technique so that effects could be achieved in the printing process that had hitherto been added in paint by hand.

Man Clasping a Hand from a Cloud (1588)

(left) The meaning of this enigmatic image by Hilliard and its obscure Latin motto is unknown. The miniature's message was probably a secret shared by the sitter and the person for whom the portrait was intended.

INDEX